HANDCRAFTED FRAMES

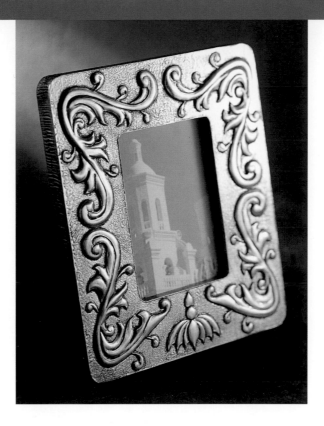

HANDCRAFTED FRAMES

Turning the Ordinary into the Extraordinary!

Compiled by Dawn Anderson

Handcrafted Frames: Turning the Ordinary
into the Extraordinary!
© 2002 Martingale & Company

The credits that appear on pages 94–95 are hereby
made a part of this copyright page.

Martingale & Company
20205 144th Avenue NE
Woodinville, WA 98072-8478
www.martingale-pub.com

Printed in Hong Kong
07 06 05 04 03 02   8 7 6 5 4 3 2 1

Library of Congress Cataloging-in-Publication data
available upon request.

ISBN: 1-56477-440-6

CREDITS
President . . . . Nancy J. Martin
CEO . . . . Daniel J. Martin
Publisher . . . . Jane Hamada
Editorial Director . . . . Mary V. Green
Managing Editor . . . . Tina Cook
Technical Editor . . . . Dawn Anderson
Copy Editor . . . . Karen Koll
Design Director . . . . Stan Green
Cover and Text Designer . . . . Jennifer LaRock Shontz

CONTENTS

INTRODUCTION

Decorative frames can be used to enhance artwork or mirrors or to hold snapshots of people and places that are special to us. This book is full of ideas for creating frames from scratch as well as for decorating existing frames. Use a single decorative frame to add a touch of whimsy to a collection of plain wood or metal frames. Or make an entire group of decorated frames for a coordinated look.

For a delicate old family photo, cover a frame in beaded tulle or checked silk fabric. Make a frame from dollhouse moldings embellished with gold leaf, jewelry chain, and beads. For a masculine look, try a cherry triptych frame, studded velvet frame, or embossed pewter frame. For a vintage look, choose from a weathered wood frame or a whitewashed ironwork frame.

The projects in this book incorporate many crafting techniques. You will find frames laminated with fabric, such as the leopard-print or floral-beaded tulle frames, and frames covered with decorative faux finishes, including a mother-of-pearl finish. Two mosaic frames are covered with shards of tile and mirror. There is also a frame covered with parquet veneer and colored stains. Whatever your previous crafting experience, you are sure to find ideas for decorating and personalizing frames for your home.

Transform an ordinary frame into a floral fantasy
with tulle, sequins, and beads.

FLORAL-BEADED TULLE FRAME

By Genevieve A. Sterbenz

Create a romantic look with ready-made rosettes and a scattering of sequins and beads over layered silk and tulle fabrics.

Turn an ordinary frame into a decorative showpiece using shiny silk fabric covered in a whisper-thin layer of tulle, beaded with sequin rosettes. The warm yellow of silk is given a peach sheen from raspberry-colored tulle; the hue deepens depending on the angle from which you view it. Sequin rosettes in shades of pink and yellow with leaves of sparkling green glisten across the frame.

Although the frame is hand beaded, premade sequin rosettes speed the process. The only techniques required to transform a piece of fabric into a blooming garden of sparkling sequins and beads are gluing, stringing beads, and a little bit of hand sewing.

The directions provided for laminating the fabric can be tailored to fit a frame of any size. Just be sure to choose a flat frame that is wide enough to showcase the beadwork. Wooden frames seem to work best, and they are inexpensive and readily available.

After you laminate the fabric to the frame, finish the raw edges with narrow satin ribbon in pink or another coordinating color. The practical solution will only enhance the frame.

For a variation on this frame, try another color scheme for the fabric and the beads. The color of the tulle overlay can greatly affect the look of the frame. You can use matching tulle for a more monochromatic look or contrasting tulle for more depth. Experiment with different colored tulles to see what appeals to you.

MATERIALS

Makes one 9" x 7" frame
½ yard yellow silk taffeta
½ yard cream cotton
½ yard raspberry tulle
9" x 7" wooden frame with 4" x 6" picture opening
Spray adhesive
High-tack white glue
¾ yard ¼"-wide raspberry satin ribbon
1 yard ⅜"-wide yellow satin ribbon
18 sequin rosettes in shades of pink (light pale pink, pastel pink, candy pink, and hot pink)
10 sequin rosettes in shades of yellow (light pale yellow, lemon yellow, butter yellow, and mustard)
One 6" length of prestrung sequins in apple green
One 6" length of prestrung seed beads in apple green
Green thread
One 6" length of prestrung sequins in candy pink
One 6" length of prestrung seed beads in lemon yellow

YOU'LL ALSO NEED:

Iron and ironing board, press cloth, kraft paper, newspaper, ruler, pencil, sharp scissors, self-healing mat, rotary cutter, small bowl, hand-sewing needle

INSTRUCTIONS

1. **Cut silk taffeta, cream cotton, and tulle rectangles.**
   Remove glass and backing from frame; set aside. Lay silk taffeta wrong side up on ironing board and press with iron to remove wrinkles. Repeat with cotton and tulle; use a press cloth when ironing tulle to prevent melting. Measure the depth (A) and width (B) of frame border. Add A and B together. Add twice this measurement to total length (C) and to total width (D) of the frame. This is the amount of fabric you will need (illustration A). Draft and cut 3 rectangles, one from silk taffeta, one from cotton, and one from tulle. Set silk taffeta and tulle aside.

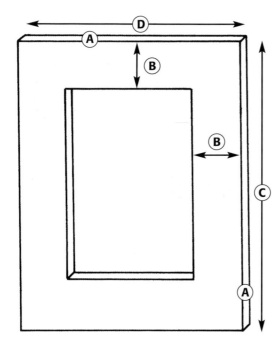

A. 2 (A + B) + C = total length of fabric needed
2 (A + B) + D = total width of fabric needed

2. **Laminate silk taffeta and cotton together.**
   Cover work surface with kraft paper. Cover a second work surface with newspaper. Place cotton, which will serve as liner, on newspaper, wrong side up. Apply light coat of spray adhesive to cotton. Carefully move cotton to kraft paper, keeping adhesive side up. Position silk taffeta, right side up, over cotton; line up edges and adhere together, smoothing flat with hands.

3. **Laminate tulle to lined silk taffeta.**
   Place laminated fabrics on kraft paper with silk taffeta facing up. Place tulle on newspaper. Hold spray adhesive at least 12" away from tulle and apply a very light coat. Turn tulle over and carefully position it over silk taffeta. Line up all edges and press down to adhere together.

4. **Laminate fabrics to frame.**
   Place laminated fabric in a vertical position, liner side up, on kraft paper. Center frame wrong side up over fabric; trace around outside and inside edges of frame with a pencil. Lift off frame and set aside. Place laminated fabric liner side up on fresh newspaper. Apply light coat of spray adhesive to fabric. Carefully move fabric to kraft paper keeping adhesive side up. Position frame wrong side up on fabric; use penciled lines as guide for placement. Bring one long side of fabric up and onto back side of frame. Smooth flat. Repeat with opposite long side. Using scissors, trim out excess fabric at corners and discard (illustration B). Fold down back flap and then side flap. Smooth fabric against frame to adhere (illustration C). Fold in corner fabric on remaining edge and cut away designated area (illustration D). Repeat at remaining 3 corners of the frame. Apply scant dabs of white glue as necessary to hold back and side flaps in place. Fold up and smooth fabric flat against frame on remaining 2 sides to adhere (illustration E).

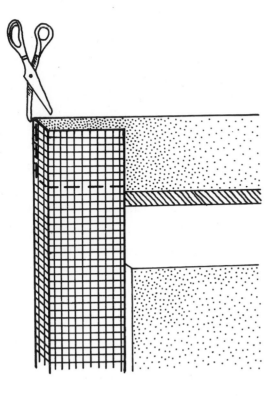

B. Fold two long edges onto frame back and trim away excess at corners.

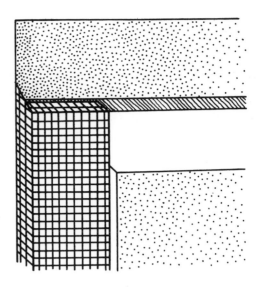

C. Fold down back and side flaps at corners.

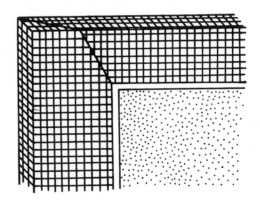

E. Fold up fabric on remaining two sides of frame, securing to frame back.

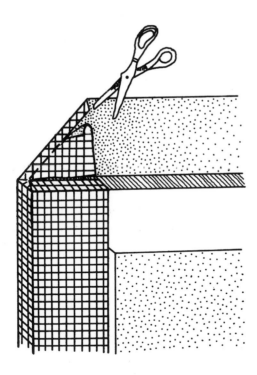

D. Trim away triangle of excess fabric at corner.

5. **Make picture opening.**

Lay frame face down on cutting mat. Using rotary cutter, cut fabric in frame opening diagonally, from corner to corner. Repeat from opposite corners to make X-shaped cut (illustration F). Use scissors to complete cuts into corners. Bring up 1 triangular flap of fabric onto inside lip of frame and just over back edge. Press to adhere and smooth flat using hands. Repeat for remaining 3 sides. Use rotary cutter to trim away excess fabric from back edge of frame on all 4 sides (illustration G).

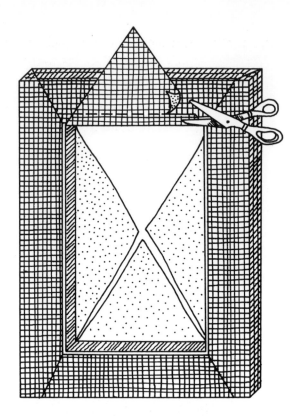

G. Fold triangular flaps to back of frame;
trim excess fabric.

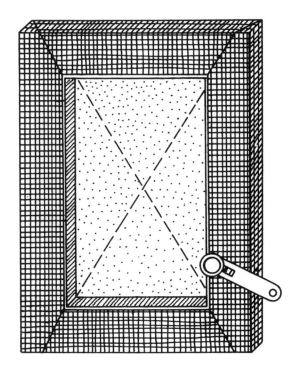

F. Cut an X through the center of the fabric
on the back side.

6. **Add raspberry satin ribbon to inside lip at picture opening.**

Using scissors, cut a 21" length of raspberry ribbon. Place frame face up on work surface. Apply dabs of white glue along one side of inside lip of frame. Position end of ribbon at corner so it covers inside lip and raw edges of fabric. Run glue and ribbon around remaining 3 inside edges. Cut ribbon at corner where ends meet; secure with glue.

7. **Add yellow satin ribbon to picture opening on back side of frame.**

Place frame wrong side up on kraft paper. Using scissors, make a clean cut at one edge of yellow ribbon. Position ribbon on right edge of frame opening ⅜" beyond corner at upper edge, covering raw edges of fabric. Trim ribbon ⅜" beyond lower corner at right edge of frame opening. Secure ribbon in place with glue. Repeat on opposite side.

Using scissors, make a 45-degree angle cut at one end of remaining ribbon length. Secure ribbon to the top and bottom edges of the frame opening in the same manner as for the sides, making diagonal cuts at ends of ribbon for mitered corners.

8. **Add sequin rosettes.**

Place frame right side up. Position 3 sequin rosettes in different shades of pink in each corner. Then, add pairs of rosettes and single rosettes in yellow and pink along sides of frame. Place rosettes in mirror image of each other on long sides of frame and in opposite positions on short sides of frame. Apply dab of white glue to underside of each rosette and then gently press in place (illustration H).

H. Glue sequin rosettes to frame front.

9. **Add sequin leaves.**

Cut the string on a prestrung length of green sequins and slide sequins off string into bowl. Thread needle and double knot the end. Insert needle into fabric at edge of 1 rosette. String on 5 green sequins, followed by a green seed bead. Repeat sequin and bead combination 2 more times. To shape leaf, try variations of stretching sequins and beads out in a straight line, curving them, or bringing needle back to original insertion site. Insert needle into fabric at desired point, tie double knot, and cut thread. Tack length of sequins and beads in place with thread or glue as desired. Add individual leaves along sides of frame by gluing down 1 green sequin, and then gluing 1 green seed bead over hole in sequin, using white glue. Add clusters of leaves as desired.

10. **Add rosebud clusters.**

Apply small dab of white glue to back of pink sequin and position on frame as desired. Apply small dab of glue to yellow seed bead and position over hole in pink sequin. Position rosebuds individually or in clusters as desired across frame surface.

11. **Add sequin rosettes at corners of picture opening on back of frame.**

Glue 1 sequin rosette to each corner of frame opening on back side over ribbon joins.

Select velvet colors and a tack arrangement that complement the photograph or artwork you plan to frame.

STUDDED VELVET FRAMES

By Mary Ann Hall

Learn how to laminate any frame with fabric, using upholstery tacks as accents.

Use scraps of velvet and a few upholstery tacks to revitalize a plain wooden frame. This simple technique is adaptable to a frame of any size, as long as the opening rim is no deeper than ¼". If it is deeper, the velvet won't adequately cover the inside corners.

If the frame has a paint or finish on it, sand it lightly with 200-grit sand-paper before you begin. If the frame is unfinished, no preparation is needed. You will need a remnant of velvet fabric that is 2" larger all around than the frame you are planning to cover. To cover the frame, lightly coat the back of the velvet with spray adhesive and lay the frame in the center. Cut out a rectangle at each corner and fold the edges around to the back of the frame, then run a rotary cutter diagonally through the overlap and remove the excess fabric to prevent the corners from bulking up.

Use upholstery tacks to complete the design. Though hardware stores generally stock a sufficient range of tack styles to choose from, you will likely find more variety at a fabric store specializing in upholstery supplies.

Plan the tack arrangement before you tap them in; make sure to position them far enough from the inner opening to clear the lip that holds the glass.

MATERIALS

Makes one frame

- Nylon or rayon velvet fabric remnant
- Flat wooden picture frame
- Spray adhesive
- Upholstery tacks

YOU'LL ALSO NEED:

Velvet board; iron; clear acrylic grid ruler; rotary cutter; self-healing cutting mat; newsprint; small, sharp scissors; hammer; 2 dozen ⅜" shirt buttons; fabric-marking pencil

INSTRUCTIONS

1. **Cut velvet rectangle.**

   Lay velvet face down on velvet board and press with cool iron to remove wrinkles. Remove glass and backing from frame; set aside. Measure frame, e.g., 7" x 9". Using rotary cutter and mat, cut rectangle from velvet 2" larger all around, e.g., 9" x 11".

2. **Adhere velvet to frame.**

   Lay velvet rectangle face down on newsprint and spray wrong side with adhesive, following manufacturer's instructions. Center frame face down on velvet and press to adhere. Fold 1 velvet edge up onto side of frame (do not fold onto back of frame). Using scissors, trim out corner rectangle at each end and discard (illustration A). Fold remainder onto back of frame and press to adhere. Repeat process on opposite edge of frame. Fold 2 remaining edges onto side and back of frame (illustration B). Use rotary cutter to cut diagonally from inside to outside corner (illustration C). To reduce bulk, remove two triangles. Butt edges to make miter join.

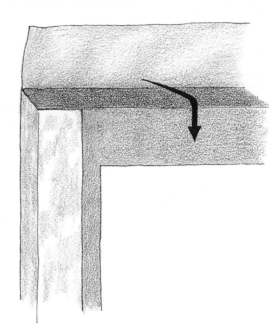

B. Fold the two remaining edges, overlapping the corners.

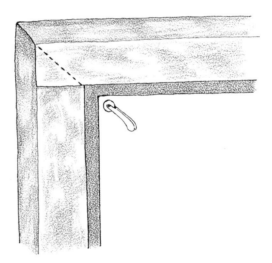

C. Miter-cut the overlapped sections and remove the surplus triangles.

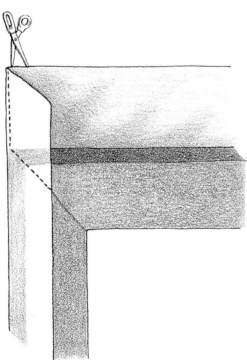

A. Fold two opposite edges onto frame and trim out the corners.

3. **Make picture opening.**

Lay frame face down on cutting mat. Using rotary cutter, cut fabric in frame opening diagonally, from corner to corner. Repeat from opposite corners to make X-shaped cut. Use scissors to complete cuts into corners. Fold 1 triangular flap up onto inside lip of frame and press to adhere. Run rotary cutter along inside edge to trim off excess. Repeat process for 3 remaining edges.

4. **Plan upholstery tack pattern.**

Lay frame right side up on flat, hard surface. Use buttons to plot upholstery tack design, experimenting with different arrangements until you create a look you like. Remove buttons, marking a dot at each location. Check placement with grid ruler to ensure symmetry. Use hammer to tap upholstery tack into frame at each dot.

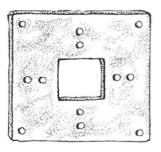

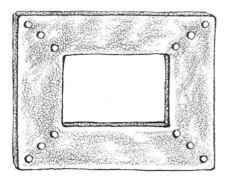

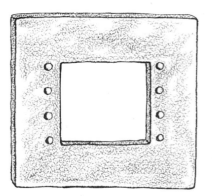

Design ideas

Frame your photograph or artwork with a double mat, selecting mat boards in colors that coordinate with the wood stains used for the frame.

MARQUETRY FRAME

By Livia McRee

Make this contemporary-looking marquetry frame easily with iron-on wood veneer.

Blocks made from wood veneer are colored with blue and green transparent stains for a bold look on a plain wood frame. The bright color and linear design give the frame a contemporary feel that works well for framing architectural pieces. You can easily change the colors of the stains to match your artwork and decor. Try classic wood-tone stains for a more neutral palette that will complement a traditional decorating style.

Veneer edging is normally used for repairing or finishing cabinets and other kinds of furniture. It is easy to use and cut, and if you purchase it pre-glued, you can iron it in place quickly and cleanly. It can be found at woodworking and home-improvement stores.

MATERIALS

Makes one 11½" x 13½" frame
11½" x 13½" unfinished wood frame with 7½" x 9½" picture opening
Iron-on veneer edging
Woodburst transparent wood stains in Phthalo Blue and Phthalo Green

YOU'LL ALSO NEED:

Pencil, clear acrylic grid ruler, self-healing cutting mat, craft knife, piece of cardboard slightly larger than frame, 2 disposable containers, cotton swabs, paper towels, kraft paper or aluminum foil, iron and ironing board

---

DESIGNER'S TIP

Make a collection of coordinating frames in various sizes, changing the placement of veneer strips on each frame for added interest.

For example, rather than alternate horizontal and vertical blocks, position strips either horizontally or vertically along the sides of the frame and miter the strips at the corners.

1. **Plan size and arrangement of blocks.**

    Remove glass and backing from frame; set aside. Draft frame dimensions onto cardboard. Using a pencil and ruler, draft lines extending edge of picture opening to outer edges of frame to make corner squares. Divide corner squares into 4 or 5 equal parts, either vertically or horizontally. My corner squares measured 2", so I divided them into four ½"-wide horizontal strips (illustration A).

    Measure space along sides of frame between corner squares and divide space into units of approximately equal size for blocks. Use an odd number of units between corner squares. If you have a square frame, the layout of the blocks can be identical on all sides. For a rectangular frame, there will be 2 different layouts, 1 for shorter sides and 1 for longer sides. I used 3 blocks on short sides and 5 blocks on long sides. Divide each block into 4 or 5 strips as for corner squares, alternating vertical and horizontal placement of strips in alternate blocks (illustration B). Also measure sides of frame on outer edge and measure inner edge of frame around picture opening for veneer strips. Record measurements for future reference.

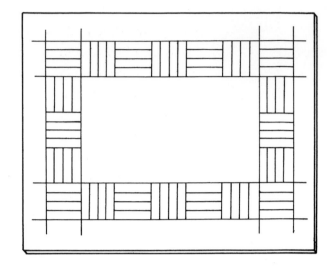

B. Divide the sides of the frame into an odd number of blocks. Divide each block into 4 or 5 strips.

2. **Cut veneer strips.**

    Using clear acrylic ruler, self-healing cutting mat, and craft knife, cut strips to size as determined in step 1. Trap veneer under ruler, and use ruler's markings as a guide to avoid having to mark veneer itself (illustration C). As you cut strips, arrange them on piece of cardboard in pattern you have sketched. Use tape to keep them from shifting.

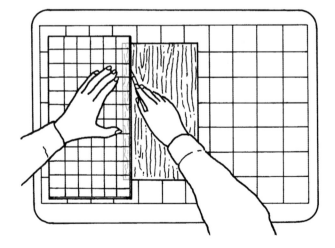

C. Cut veneer strips using a craft knife and ruler.

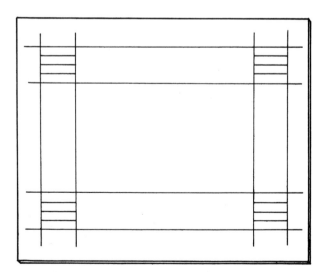

A. Draw squares at corners of frame and divide each square into 4 or 5 strips.

3. **Stain veneer strips.**

Following manufacturer's instructions, shake stain and pour a little of each color into separate disposable containers. Using cotton swab, apply stain to wood veneer, following wood grain. Stain strips, alternating between green and blue. Wipe stain with paper towel until you achieve desired translucency. If you want a more opaque look, wait for stain to dry 24–48 hours and apply another coat. As you stain strips, replace them on cardboard pattern. Be sure to alternate between blue and green consistently (illustration D).

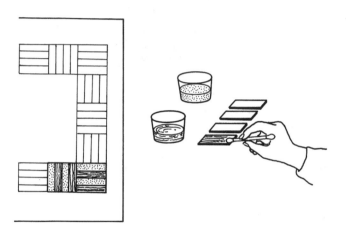

D. Apply stain to wood strips using a cotton swab.

Stain strips for inner and outer edges as for other strips, using blue stain. Wait 24–48 hours for stain to completely dry. You should not be able to rub off any stain with a paper towel.

4. **Iron veneer strips in place.**

Preheat iron on cotton setting. Use a piece of kraft paper or aluminum foil to protect bottom of iron. Following manufacturer's directions, iron veneer strips in place. Burnish strips down with your fingers while glue is still warm. If you make a mistake, reheat strip to shift or remove it. Continue to adhere strips to frame in desired pattern. Iron veneer strips to inner and outer edges of frame in same manner.

For a variation on this two-tone graphic design, cut
the triangles, parallelograms, and trapezoids from
several different colors of paper.

FAUX EBONY AND IVORY MARQUETRY FRAME

By Lily Franklin

Transform an unfinished wooden frame into an old-world masterpiece using cut paper and a simple decoupage technique.

In designing this marquetry frame, I set out to simulate the look of inlaid ebony and ivory using everyday materials. After some experimentation, I ended up painting a wooden frame black, then decoupaging pieces of ivory-colored paper in a repeating pattern. The resulting design is boldly graphic, with a classic contrast.

To start off, I added narrow three-dimensional rims along the inside and outside edges of my flat frame. These rims, cut from basswood strips, create a natural enclosure for the inlaid paper. After I glued the basswood rims in place, I sanded and painted the frame.

I found that several paper characteristics are key to simulating inlaid ivory. First and foremost, the paper must be thick enough to remain opaque after it is decoupaged in place. If the paper is so thin that it becomes translucent during decoupage, the black paint will show through and the inlay will appear gray and dull. To test a paper's opacity, wet it and press it against a dark background. It should remain a strong off-white color, be stiff for easy handling, and be free from warping. A second characteristic is surface texture: Your paper should be smooth, without any pebbly or laid textures to mar the illusion of inlaid ivory.

Most of the graphic pattern on the frame is created with one basic shape: the parallelogram. To make identical parallelograms, I employed a simple geometric formula. The width of the parallelogram is exactly one-half of the width of the area to be inlaid. The corners are filled in with triangles, which are parallelograms trimmed to fit. All the pieces can be cut from a single 8½" x 11½" sheet of paper.

MATERIALS

Makes one 11" x 14" frame
11" x 14" unfinished wood frame
Eight ³⁄₁₆" x ³⁄₁₆" x 24" basswood sticks
8½" x 11" sheet ivory parchment paper
2 ounces flat black acrylic craft paint
Mod Podge, gloss-lustré finish
Sanding sealer
Acrylic sealer
Wood glue

YOU'LL ALSO NEED:

Clear acrylic grid ruler, pencil, craft knife, self-healing cutting mat, sponge, heavy books, newsprint, small wood blocks, soap, 220-grit sandpaper, paper towels, steel ruler, steel triangle, soft ½"-wide flat brush, 400-grit wet-dry emery paper

INSTRUCTIONS

1. **Mark frame for basswood rims.**

   Remove glass and backing from frame; set aside. Using grid ruler and pencil, draft guidelines on face of frame ¼" from each outer edge and ⅜" from each inner edge (see illustration A). Measure and jot down the perpendicular distance between the 2 lines at X and the diagonal distance between the lines at corner Y.

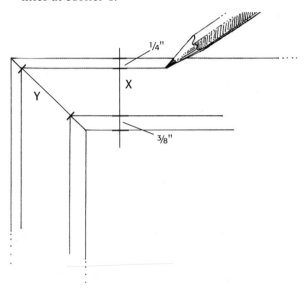

   A. Draft guidelines along the frame's inner and outer edges. Measure and record X and Y.

2. **Miter-cut and glue basswood rims.**

   Align basswood on outer edge of ¼" line so ends extend beyond frame miter (illustration B). At each end, press craft-knife blade into stick at 45-degree angle, using frame miter as guide. Then transfer stick to cutting mat and cut clear through. Repeat to miter-cut 8 strips total, 1 for each inner and outer edge of frame. Apply wood glue to bottom of each stick and to marked areas on frame, and then glue sticks to frame to create raised rims along inner and outer edges of frame. When all sticks are glued in place, double-check that corners are square. Wipe oozing glue with damp sponge. Weight evenly with heavy books and let dry at least 1 hour, but preferably overnight.

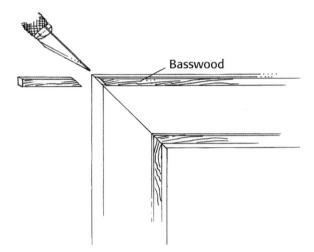

   B. Miter the corners of eight basswood sticks and glue them in place.

3. **Paint frame.**

   Protect work surface with newsprint. Prop frame on small blocks to prevent sticking, and then brush light coat of sanding sealer over front and back of frame. Clean brush with soap and water. Let frame dry 1 hour. Sand lightly with 220-grit sandpaper wrapped around small wood block; then wipe off dust using damp paper towel. Brush on black paint and let dry 20 minutes. Apply second coat. Clean brush with soap and water. Let frame dry 24 hours.

4. Cut parchment parallelograms.

Divide X measurement from step 1 in half. Measuring from left edge of parchment, mark off this amount evenly spaced across top and bottom edges. Lay steel ruler across parchment to connect marks; then cut parchment with craft knife, stopping just short of edges (illustration C) Divide Y measurement from step 1 in half. Measuring from top left corner of parchment, mark off this amount evenly spaced across top edge and down left edge. Lay steel ruler across paper diagonally to connect marks, and cut with craft knife from edge to edge until you have about forty parallelograms (illustration D, #1). Align steel triangle on excess strips to cut four right-angle triangles (illustration D, #2). Set aside remaining strips.

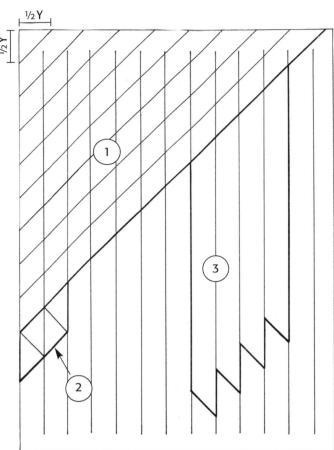

D. Use the Y measure to make diagonal cuts for (1) parallelograms, (2) triangles, and (3) trapezoids.

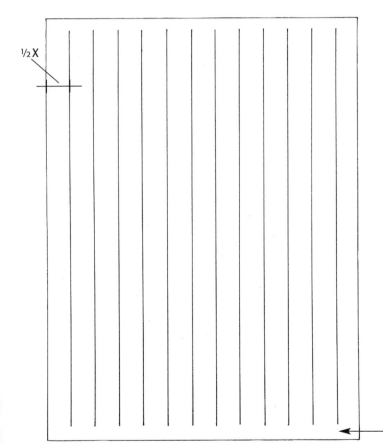

C. Use the X measure to cut vertical strips on the sheet of parchment. Stop just short of the edges.

5. Glue parallelograms to frame.

Test-fit pieces on frame, placing one triangle at corner and four parallelograms along each side between basswood rims (illustration E). Remove pieces from frame and set on newsprint. Brush moderately thick coat of Mod Podge across triangle and onto newsprint to fully coat edges. Beginning at frame corner, press triangle into position and smooth to remove air bubbles. Working out from corner, glue on four parallelograms one by one. Repeat to decorate all four corners. To fill each middle area, cut four trapezoidal strips from excess paper in step 4 (illustration D, #3). To cut correct length, position one strip on frame so angled end touches point of parallelogram (illustration F). Make tick mark at other end. Then cut angle using scrap parallelogram as guide. Double-check strip length, and then glue in place.

E. Starting at each corner, glue 1 triangle and 4 parallelograms in place.

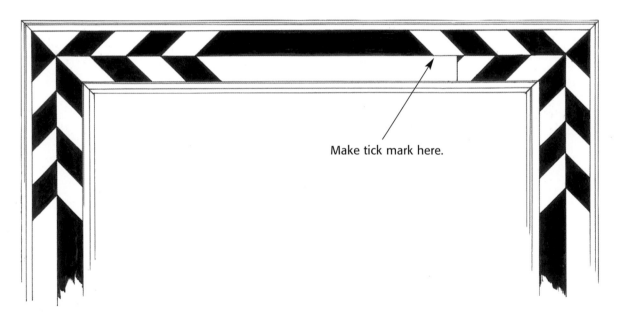

Make tick mark here.

F. Mark and angle-cut a long trapezoid to span each middle section.

6. **Coat frame with Mod Podge.**

Brush light coat of Mod Podge over face of frame and let dry 20 minutes. Sand lightly with 400-grit wet-dry emery paper. To build finish, repeat at least four more times or until surface is even. Let dry overnight. To eliminate tackiness, apply acrylic sealer (illustration G).

G. Coat the frame face with four layers of Mod Podge, and then apply acrylic sealer.

Mirror shards add sharp contrast to the frame. For less contrast, substitute a fourth tile color for the mirrored sections.

MOSAIC MIRROR FRAME

By Jill MacKay

This mosaic mirror makes a great weekend project. You will find it relatively easy, even if this is your first experience with mosaics. I used a wood frame with a wide, flat surface as the base for this design. I chose three shades of blue tiles to mimic the colors of water and combined the tile shards with sparkling mirror shards for contrast. You can easily substitute other tile colors to customize the mirror to your own decor.

The tiles I used are sold in craft stores and you can also buy them online (see Sources on page 93). I used ceramic tile nippers to break the glass tiles into shards with jagged edges. Then I used mosaic cutters to trim any tile shards to precise shapes in order to make the pieces fit the pattern. Protect your eyes at all times with safety goggles when cutting tiles and mirror, as some tiles may shatter. To create the mosaic design, the broken tiles are glued in place on the wood frame base in the desired design, and then grout is applied over the tiles to fill in the cracks.

You will find that fitting the odd shaped tile shards together gets easier the more you do it. You develop an eye for it. You'll see the shape you need and this will mean less nipping and shaping. It's like putting a puzzle together and looking for the right shaped piece.

For a professional look, always glue tiles and mirror flush with the edge of the frame. Do not let anything extend out over the edge. This will also give you nice, straight grout lines. Whenever possible put the smooth, finished edge of the tile facing toward the outer edge of the frame.

MATERIALS

Makes one 18" x 18" frame

4 oz. Plaid Folk Art Outdoor Brilliant Gloss Sealer
18" x 18" wood frame with an 8"x 8" picture opening
12" x 12" square mirror
Mosaic Mercantile Vitreous Glass Tile in the following colors:
    1-lb. bag Rainwater
    1-lb. bag Tide and ½-lb. bag Tide
    1-lb. bag Lagoon
8½" x 8½" mirror, with or without 1" bevel
2 lb. white sanded grout

YOU'LL ALSO NEED:

Pattern (page 35), use of photocopy machine, graphite paper, dull pencil, 1 sheet 19" x 24" tracing paper (or 5 sheets 8.5" x 11" tracing paper), marker, hand-held glass cutter, safety goggles, breaking pliers, running pliers, 5 paper plates, silicone glue, old paintbrush, mosaic cutters, tile nippers, 12 oz. Weldbond adhesive, plastic drop cloth, razor blade, masking tape, 2 disposable containers or small buckets, rubber gloves, sponge, soft polishing cloth (not terry-cloth), large tweezers

INSTRUCTIONS

1. **Prepare frame and pattern.**

   Brush a coat of sealer over entire front surface of frame (including edges). Let dry for 30 minutes and then repeat. Turn frame over and apply 1 coat of sealer to back; let dry. Enlarge pattern on page 35 on a photocopy machine. Place graphite paper over 1 corner of the frame front with the pattern on top, aligning edge of pattern with edge of frame. Using a dull pencil, transfer design to the corner of the frame. The spirals mirror each other, creating a symmetrical design. Turn your photocopied pattern over and hold it up to a window, and trace the design onto the backside of paper. This way you can flip and rotate the pattern as needed. Once design is transferred, go over graphite lines with marker so they are easier to see.

2. **Cut and apply mirror shards to frame.**

   Wear safety goggles. Score fourteen 12" strips of mirror ½" wide with glass cutter. Then score again across the strips at ¾" intervals to create ½" x ¾" rectangles. Using the breaking pliers, snap off each 12"-long strip. Then, carefully holding each strip over a paper plate, snap off each individual rectangle until you finish all strips. Apply silicone glue to outer edge of frame. Secure mirror rectangles to edge, being careful to fit pieces flush with edge of frame. Repeat for remaining 3 outer edges and then repeat for inner edges of frame. Using mosaic cutters, cut remaining rectangles of mirror into smaller odd-shaped pieces (shards), nipping 2–4 pieces from each ½" x ¾" rectangle. Fill in each corner section marked as "A" one at a time by gluing mirror pieces in place with Weldbond adhesive, nipping with mosaic cutters to fit. Use tweezers to help position small pieces in place. Glue mirror shards onto the 4 strips marked as "A" that run between the 4 spirals (illustration A).

A. Glue mirror shards in place.

3. Cut and apply tile shards to frame.

Using tile nippers, break up ⅔ of 1-lb. bag of Rainwater tiles onto a paper plate. Break tiles into as many different shapes as possible. Apply Rainwater tile shards to one "B" section at a time. Cover area to be tiled with Weldbond adhesive and then begin filling in, shaping pieces with mosaic cutters when necessary. Where possible, lay smooth, finished edge of tile along edge of frame.

Use tile nippers to break up 1-lb. bag of Tide tiles. You will use more than a pound, but it's nice to leave a few whole tiles in every color in case you want to cut a tile to fill a particular space. Carefully fill in the 4 main spirals (marked as "C") with Tide tile, gluing a section of each spiral at a time. Shape pieces to fit as necessary, using the mosaic cutters. Pay close attention to your placement, staying right on the line so all spirals look exactly the same size. Use the tile nippers to break up nearly the whole bag of Lagoon tile, leaving a few tiles whole. Working on 1 section at a time, secure Lagoon tile shards to the areas marked as "D"; place the finished edge of tiles along inner edge of frame at opening for mirror (illustration B). Let dry overnight.

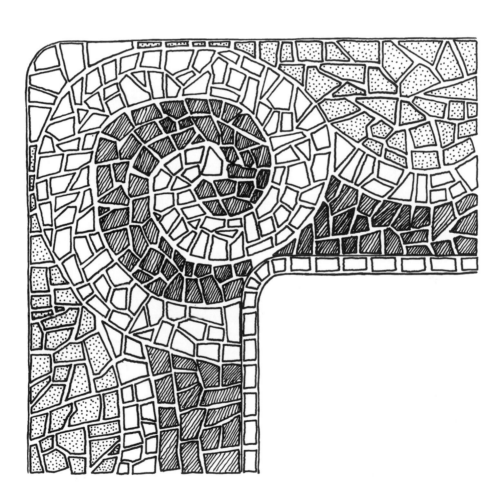

B. Fill in sections with tile shards.

4. **Secure mirror to frame.**

    Place a plastic drop cloth on a flat surface. Turn frame face down. Run bead of silicone glue, approximately ¼" wide, around recessed edge of frame. Place 8½" x 8½" mirror face down into place. Run another bead of glue around back edge of mirror. Holding glue container vertically and touching frame, force glue down into small gap between frame and mirror. Place something that weighs a pound or two onto backside of mirror to hold it in place while drying; let dry. Turn frame face up. Using a razor blade, carefully clean off any dried glue from tiles and mirror.

5. **Apply grout.**

    Prepare to grout by masking off mirror. Run a strip of masking tape right up next to frame edge, being careful not to go beneath any mosaic work. Continue masking until entire surface of mirror is covered. Cover table with plastic. Fill 1 bucket with water and put approximately 1½ lbs. of grout into other bucket. Following manufacturer's instructions, mix grout thoroughly. Apply grout over entire surface, using gloved fingertips to push grout into crevices (illustration C). Carefully fill the spaces between face of frame and edges. Use fingertip to smooth these grout lines. Let grout set up for 10–15 minutes. Wet sponge in water, wringing out the excess. Sponge away excess grout, but be careful not to remove too much. You may need to go back and fix grout lines where top and sides meet if small amounts of grout become dislodged by sponge. Let dry another 15–20 minutes; polish clean using soft cloth.

C. Apply grout over surface.

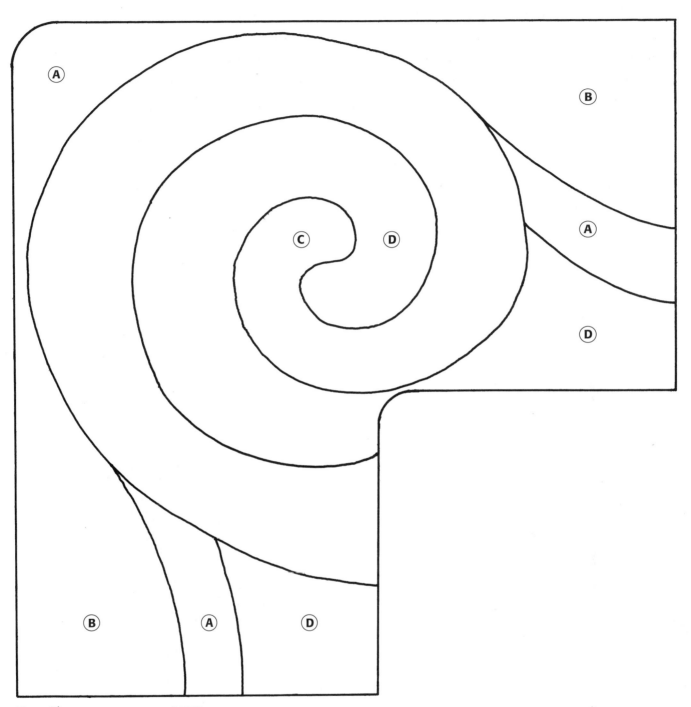

Note: Photocopy pattern at 133%.

Color Key

A = Mirror

B = Rainwater

C = Tide

D = Lagoon

For a custom look, select the photograph or artwork you wish to frame first. Then select tile colors that coordinate with the colors of the chosen piece.

MOSAIC PICTURE FRAME

By Jill MacKay

This glass tile and mirror picture frame is whimsical in its design.

The mirror used for this project is easily cut with a glass cutter. The glass tile can be cut with tile nippers or mosaic cutters. For precise shaping, the pieces can be further trimmed with mosaic cutters to fit the pattern. Protect your eyes at all times with safety goggles when cutting tiles and mirror; they can shatter. To create the mosaic design, glue the broken tiles in place on the wood frame, following the marked design lines, and then apply grout over the tiles to fill in the cracks.

Always glue tile and mirror shards flush with the edges of the frame. Do not let anything extend out over the edges. This also gives you nice, straight grout lines on the inner and outer edges of the frame. Whenever possible face the smooth, finished edge of the tile toward the frame's edges.

Breaking pliers, glass cutters, and mosaic cutters can also be purchased at any stained-glass supply store.

DESIGNER'S TIP

Sanded grout is available in a variety of colors. You may wish to coordinate your grout color and tile colors for less contrast between the tile shards.

MATERIALS

Makes one 12¼" x 12¼" frame

12¼" x 12¼" plain wooden frame with 5" x 7" picture opening

4 oz. Plaid Folk Art Outdoor Brilliant Gloss Sealer

12" x 12" square mirror

Mosaic Mercantile Vitreous Glass Tile in the following colors:

    1-lb. bag Tide

    ½-lb. bag Rainwater

    2 lb. white sanded grout

YOU'LL ALSO NEED:

Pattern (page 41), ½" flat paint brush, graphite paper, dull pencil, 1 sheet 12" x 14" tracing paper, bold-point black permanent marker, ruler, safety glasses, hand-held glass cutter, breaking pliers, 3 paper plates, silicone glue, old paintbrush, 8 oz. Weldbond adhesive, mosaic cutters, tile nippers, razor blade, plastic drop cloth, 2 disposable containers or small buckets, rubber gloves, sponge, soft polishing cloth (not terry-cloth)

INSTRUCTIONS

1. Prepare pattern and frame.

Remove glass and backing from frame; set aside. Brush coat of sealer over entire front surface of frame (including edges), let dry for 30 minutes, and then repeat. Turn frame over and apply 1 coat of sealer to back; let dry. Enlarge pattern on page 41 on a photocopy machine. Place graphite paper over the frame front with the pattern on top, aligning edges of pattern with edges of frame. Using a dull pencil, transfer design to the frame. Once the design is transferred, go over graphite lines with marker so they are easier to see.

2. Cut mirror shards and apply to outer edges.

Put on safety glasses. Score four 12" strips of mirror, ⅜" wide, using glass cutter. Then score across strips at ¾" intervals to score ⅜" x ¾" rectangles. Using breaking pliers, snap off each of the 12" long strips. Then, carefully holding each strip over a paper plate, snap off each ⅜" x ¾" rectangle. Apply the silicone glue to 1 side edge of frame. Secure mirror rectangles to edge of frame so they are flush with edge. Repeat on remaining 3 sides, applying glue to 1 side at a time. Score five 12" strips of mirror, ¾" wide. Then score across the strips at ¾" intervals to score ¾" x ¾" squares. Using the breaking pliers, snap off each of the 12" long strips. Then, carefully holding each strip over a paper plate, snap off each ¾" x ¾" square. Using tile nippers, cut each square into smaller shards in a variety of shapes and sizes. Cut some squares only once and cut some into as many as 4 pieces.

3. Apply mirror shards to frame front.

Following pattern and tile placement diagram on page 40, and using Weldbond adhesive, glue mirror shards into place. Shape pieces with mosaic cutters to fit where necessary. Finish all sections to be filled with mirror shards. Make sure no mirror shards extend out over the edge of the frame; glue them flush with edge of frame to create straight grout lines (illustration A).

A. Glue mirror shards in place.

4.   Cut and apply tile shards to frame.

Use mosaic cutters to cut almost entire bag of Rainwater tiles into thirds. Turn the tiles over and cut parallel with the lines on the back. Cut each tile twice, creating 3 strips approximately ¼" wide. Glue Rainwater strips around edges of each mirrored section. Use mosaic cutter to shape where necessary. When curving around rounded end of mirror shapes, nip series of smaller pieces (see tile placement diagram) to shape smooth curve. Cut almost entire bag of Tide tiles into shards of different shapes using tile nippers. Finish covering surface of frame by gluing on Tide tile shards. Try to remember to place finished edge of tile so that it faces out on both the inside and outside edges of frame.

5. Cut and apply mirror tiles to inner edge of frame. Score three 12" strips of mirror ¼" wide. Then score across strips at ¾" intervals to score ¼" x ¾" rectangles. Using breaking pliers, snap off each 12" long strip. Then, carefully holding each strip over a paper plate, snap off each individual ¼" x ¾" rectangle. Cut 4 rectangles into fourths. These small squares will be used for inside corners. Glue mirror rectangles along inside edge of frame, making sure to position them carefully so they are flush with front and back edges, or the glass that covers the photo will no longer fit flat into the frame. Glue small squares of mirror along each side of the inside corners (illustration B). Let dry overnight.

B. Glue mirror strips to inner edge of frame.

6. Apply grout.

Using razor blade, carefully remove any dried glue from surface of mirror and glass tile. Cover table with plastic. Fill 1 bucket with water and put approximately 1¼ lb. grout into other bucket. Following manufacturer's instructions, mix grout thoroughly. Apply grout over entire surface, using gloved fingertips to push grout down into crevices. Carefully fill spaces between top and edges. Use fingertip to smooth these grout lines. Let grout set up for 10–15 minutes. Wet sponge in water, wringing out excess. Sponge away excess grout, but be careful not to remove too much. You may need to go back and fix the grout lines where the top and side edges meet if small amounts of grout are dislodged by the sponge. Let dry another 15 to 20 minutes and then polish clean with a soft cloth.

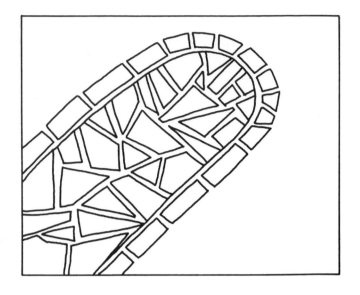

Tile placement diagram

Danish oil brings out the color and detail of the
cherry grain while retaining a natural "dry wood"
finish.

CHERRY TRIPTYCH FRAME

By Sandra Salamony

Use simple hardware and a piece of wood to create a freestanding display for three favorite photos.

This triptych frame is perfect for showcasing any group of three: children in candid poses, a few generations of wedding portraits, a set of picture postcards, or even vacation photos shot as a panorama. The protective glass panels are held in place with brass pins but slide out easily when you want to change the images.

The frame itself is made of solid cherry sawed into three panels. You can cut the wood yourself if you have power tools, or you can have a woodworking shop do it for you. Be sure to arrange the wood pieces in order when you're ready to add the hinges so that the grain of the wood can flow uninterrupted. To tone down shiny bright hardware, I used Darkening Solution. Just immerse the hardware in the solution and let it sit until the desired color is obtained.

MATERIALS
Makes 1 frame
7½" x 18" x ¾" cherry plank
Danish oil (for natural finish)
Two 2½" x 2" mission-style
   hinges
Three 4" x 6" pieces of picture
   glass
Three 4" x 6" photos or images
51 brass escutcheon pins
Rockler Woodworking
   Darkening Solution

YOU'LL ALSO NEED:
Saw; drill; 220-grit sandpaper; soft, lint-free cloth; 4" x 6" cardboard template; pencil; small glass jar; hammer; screwdriver; ruler; tweezers; paper towels

INSTRUCTIONS

1. **Finish wood panels.**

   Saw 18" cherry plank into three 6"-wide panels (or have supplier do this for you). Sand edges smooth. Following manufacturer's instructions, apply Danish oil with soft cloth, let penetrate 5 minutes, and then wipe off excess. Repeat after 24 hours. Let dry 24 hours.

2. **Mark wood panels.**

   Lay 3 wood panels flat, side by side, with wood grain matching. Mark 3 edges of cardboard template in 1" increments (omit 1 short edge for top opening). Position template on center wood panel, ½" from top edge and evenly spaced on each side. Mark 17 dots on panel at template marks and corners (illustration A). Repeat to mark remaining

   panels. Center hinge over each join, separating the panels about ⅜" to clear the hinge pin. Mark and drill starter holes for hinge screws.

3. **Antique the brass pins.**

   Following package directions, pour Darkening Solution into glass jar and add brass pins. When desired color is achieved, remove pins from solution, rinse with water, and dry.

4. **Attach the pins and hinges.**

   At each marked dot, tap brass pin partway into wood so that ¼" remains visible. Repeat for each panel. Screw hinges in place to join the panels (illustration B). Slide photos and glass into the U created by the nails.

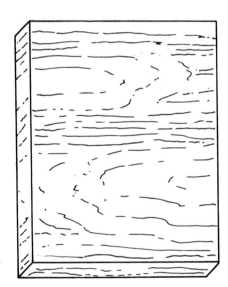 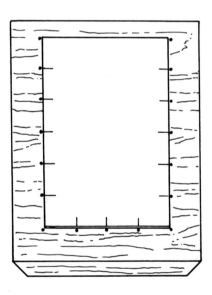 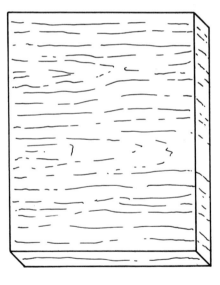

A. Mark 17 dots on center panel at template marks and corners.

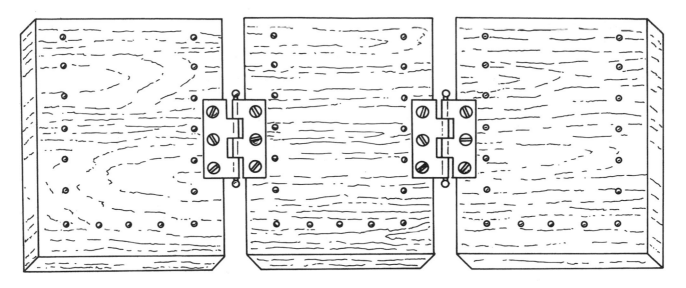

B. Tap brass pins into place at marked dots and attach hinges.

DESIGNER'S TIP

• For a distressed look, assemble this frame from "found" wood and salvaged hardware.

• Experiment with different hardware. For example, you might mount the glass with glass retainers instead of escutcheon pins. Glass retainers, sold to hold the glass in screen doors, are available at most hardware stores.

Age a handmade wooden frame with a weathered crackle finish.

WEATHERED WOOD FRAME

By Patty Cox

You can turn a handmade frame into a vintage-looking piece with a little paint and some weathered crackle glaze. I made the width of the frame larger on the bottom to accommodate a drawer pull that can be used for hanging small items such as keys or jewelry.

I painted my frame with a soft aqua and yellow to give it a beach feeling, and I chose a glass drawer pull. You can easily substitute other colors or replace the glass knob to match your own decorating style. For a masculine look in an office, try black paint over brown and then replace the drawer pull with a blackened silver hook. Or for a feminine look in a powder room, use cream paint over tan and hang a strand of pearls or a locket on the glass knob.

The frame itself is constructed from basswood boards, available at craft and hobby stores. The boards are easily cut with a craft-and-hobby miter box and saw. Once the frame pieces are cut to size, they are glued together with wood glue. Then a recessed area is created on the back of the frame for holding the acetate, photo, and backing board. I simply used thumbtacks around the outer edges on the back side to hold the pieces in place.

The patina finish is created with a base coat of paint, followed by a layer of weathered crackle glaze. Finally a topcoat of paint is applied over the crackle medium. As the paint dries, the cracks become visible.

MATERIALS

Makes one 9⅝" x 9⅝" frame
Precut basswood boards in the following sizes:
  2½" x ⅜" x 36"
  3½" x ⅜" x 36"
  ½" x ⅛" x 36"
Wood glue
DecoArt Americana acrylic paint in the following colors:
  Taffy Cream
  Sea Aqua
  Mint Julep Green
Weathered crackle glaze
1"- wide clear glass drawer knob, with screw and nut
Sawtooth picture hanger
4⅞" x 5⅞" piece of cardboard or foamcore board
4⅞" x 5⅞" piece of acetate

YOU'LL ALSO NEED:

Miter box and saw, clamps, sanding block, tack cloth, ruler, drill and ⅛" drill bit, 3 thumbtacks, pencil, disposable dish, hammer, screwdriver, X-Acto knife, 3 foam applicators

INSTRUCTIONS

1. **Construct frame.**

   Cut 2½"-wide and 3½"-wide basswood boards into lengths as shown (illustration A); use a miter box to ensure 90-degree cuts. Glue frame sides to frame top and bottom with wood glue. Hold glued wood together with clamps until dry. Remove clamps and sand edges. On frame back, draw a rectangle ⅝" larger than frame opening. From the ½" x ⅛" x 36" basswood strip, cut 2 pieces 7" long for the top and bottom of the frame and 2 pieces 5" long for the sides of the frame. Glue the strips along the edges of the drawn lines to create a recessed area for holding the photo (illustration B). Allow glue to dry. Remove debris from wood using a tack cloth.

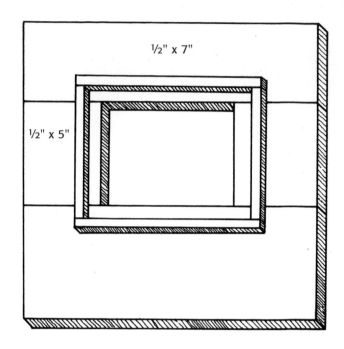

B. Glue wood strips around frame opening on back side to create recessed area for holding photo.

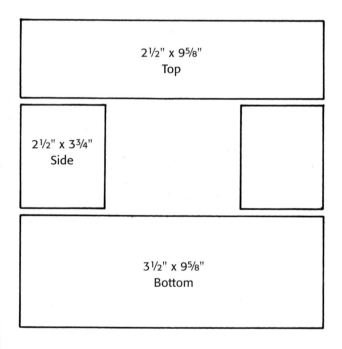

A. Cut frame pieces and secure with glue.

2. **Apply crackle finish to frame.**

   Apply base coat of Taffy Cream acrylic paint to frame front and back, and allow paint to dry completely. Generously apply weathered crackle glaze on base-coated wood. Allow crackle glaze to dry 1 to 2 hours. Mix equal amounts of Sea Aqua and Mint Julep Green in a disposable dish. Apply mixed paint over crackle glaze. Do not overwork paint. Allow paint to dry and crack.

3. Finish frame.

Measure and mark center of frame bottom. Drill an ⅛" hole in frame at marked point. Screw glass knob on frame, securing with screw and nut (illustration C). Attach sawtooth picture hanger to center back of frame along upper edge, using hammer. Using an X-Acto knife, cut a 4⅞" x 5⅞" piece of acetate and cardboard or foamcore board for backing board. Insert acetate, photo and backing board into recessed area on frame back. Insert three thumb-tacks in wood sides to secure pieces in place.

C. Secure glass knob at center bottom of frame.

TIP

If you are using a glass drawer pull to accent the frame, rub the screw with paint that matches the topcoat of paint on the frame.

The pretty colors of this silk fabric complement the soft colors of the photograph. Try a neutral checked fabric with black-and-white or sepia-tone photos.

CHECKED-SILK FRAME

By Genevieve A. Sterbenz

Use a pretty checked silk and a floral trim to give a soft look to an ordinary wood frame.

Make an old frame new again using scraps of fabric and pretty trim. Here I have covered an 8" x 10" flat-front wooden frame with a checked taffeta fabric and coordinating trim to create a feminine accent for any dressing table, living-room side table or fireplace mantel that displays an array of family photographs.

The process is easy. Measure and cut a scrap of silk taffeta fabric, laminate it to a liner fabric, and then glue it to a wooden frame with spray adhesive. The romantic trims complement the soft, sweet colors of the patterned fabric and delineate the shape of the frame. These satin ribbons and rosebud accents also make covering any imperfect raw edges practically foolproof. Here, I have used a silk check in baby blue, moss green, cream, gold, and raspberry pink in combination with satin ribbon in the same green and blue, and a shaped trim with pink roses and diminutive green leaves. This laminating technique produces such beautiful results and is so simple that you need only an hour or two to make an exquisite fabric-covered frame.

Feel free to choose whatever fabric appeals to you. For a more masculine looking frame, coordinate pin striped or suiting fabrics in wool with grosgrain ribbon in black or gray. If you use a thin fabric, line it with a second layer of fabric, such as muslin. Using a lining will prevent the possibility of a thinner fabric tearing at the corners. I chose a cream cotton liner fabric for this frame, because it did not show through the checked taffeta.

To determine the amount of fabric you need, add twice the measurement of the frame width and frame depth at the outer edge to the total length of the frame to find the length of the fabric needed. Then add twice the measurement of the frame width and frame depth at the outer edge to the total width of the frame to find the width of the fabric needed. For example, start with a frame that is 8" by 10" and has a picture opening that is 5" by 7". If the width of the wooden frame from the outside edge to the inside edge is 1½" and the depth of the frame is ½", then add 4" (1½" + ½" = 2" x 2 = 4") to the total length and width, resulting in a 12" by 14" rectangle of fabric.

MATERIALS

Makes one 8" x 10" frame

½ yard of checked silk taffeta

½ yard cream cotton fabric

8" x 10" wooden frame with 5" x 7" picture opening

Spray adhesive

High-tack white glue

2 yards ⅜"-wide moss green satin ribbon

1¼ yards ⅜"-wide chenille-style rosebud trim, in pastel pink and green

1 yard ¼"-wide pastel blue satin ribbon

YOU'LL ALSO NEED:

Iron and ironing board, ruler, pencil, sharp scissors, kraft paper, newspaper, self-healing mat, rotary cutter

INSTRUCTIONS

1. **Cut taffeta and cotton rectangles.**

   Lay taffeta wrong side up on ironing board and press with iron to remove wrinkles. Repeat with cotton. Remove glass and backing from frame; set aside. Measure the depth (A) and width (B) of frame border. Add A and B together. Add this measurement to total length (C) and to total width (D) of the frame. This is the amount of fabric you will need. Measure, mark, and cut 2 rectangles, 1 from taffeta and 1 from cotton, using ruler, pencil, and scissors (illustration A). Set taffeta aside.

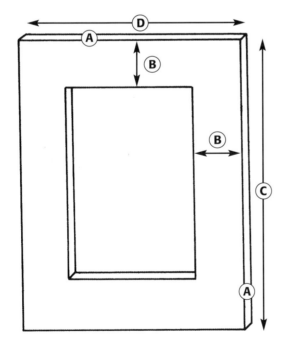

   A. 2 (A + B) + C = total length of fabric needed
   2 (A + B) + D = total width of fabric needed

2. **Laminate fabrics together.**

   Cover work surface with kraft paper. Cover a second work surface with newspaper. Place cotton liner on newspaper, wrong side up. Apply light coat of spray adhesive to cotton. Carefully move cotton to kraft paper keeping glued side up. Position taffeta, right side up, over cotton fabric. Line up edges and adhere taffeta and cotton together, smoothing flat with hands.

3. **Laminate fabric to frame.**

   Place laminated fabric, liner side up, on kraft paper. Center frame wrong side up on fabric. Trace around outside and inside edges of frame with pencil. Lift off frame and set aside. Place laminated fabric, liner side up, on clean newspaper. Apply light coat of spray adhesive to fabric. Carefully move fabric to kraft paper keeping glued side up. Position frame wrong side up on fabric, using penciled lines as guide for placement. Bring 1 long side of fabric up onto back side of frame. Smooth flat. Repeat with opposite long side. Using scissors, trim out excess fabric at corners and discard (illustration B). Fold down back flap and then side flap. Smooth fabric against frame to adhere (illustration C). Fold in corner fabric on remaining edge and cut away designated area (illustration D). Repeat at remaining 3 corners of the frame. Apply scant dabs of white glue on inside flaps that were folded over to secure in place. Fold up and smooth fabric flat against frame on remaining 2 sides to adhere (illustration E).

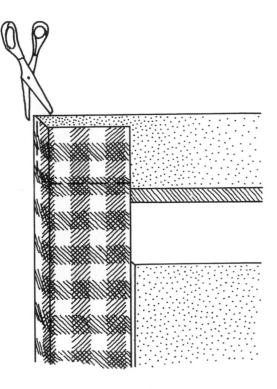

B. Fold two long edges onto frame back and trim away excess at corners.

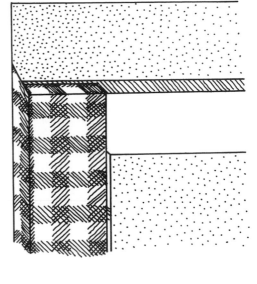

C. Fold down back and side flaps at corners.

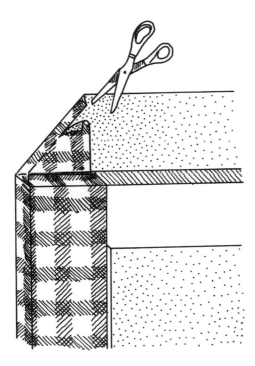

D. Trim away triangle of excess fabric at corner.

E. Fold up fabric on remaining two sides of frame, securing to frame back.

checked-silk frame

4. **Make picture opening.**

Place frame face down on cutting mat. Using rotary cutter, cut fabric in frame opening diagonally from corner to corner. Repeat from opposite corners to make X-shaped cut (illustration F). Use scissors to complete cuts into corners. Bring up 1 triangular flap of fabric onto inside lip of frame. Press to adhere and smooth flat using hands. Repeat for remaining 3 sides. Use rotary cutter to trim away excess fabric from inside edge on all 4 sides (illustration G).

G. Fold triangular flaps to back of frame; trim excess fabric.

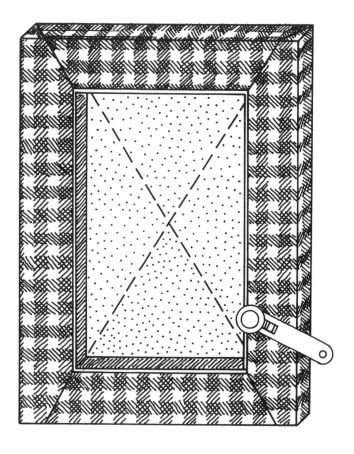

F. Cut an X through the center of the fabric on the back side.

5. **Add moss green satin ribbon.**

Place frame face up on kraft paper. Using scissors, make a clean cut at end of ribbon. Apply dabs of white glue along outer ⅜" of frame at lower edge. Position ribbon over glued area so left edge of ribbon is flush with left edge of frame. Trim ribbon flush with frame on right edge. Repeat along top edge of frame. Using scissors, make a diagonal cut at one end of remaining ribbon. Secure ribbon to the remaining sides of frame opening in the same manner, making diagonal cuts at ends of ribbon for mitered corners.

6. **Add rosebud trim.**

   Using scissors, cut trim exposing rosebud at end. Glue trim along inner edge of green satin ribbon trim, pivoting at corners (illustration H). Cut trim where ends meet and tack down with glue.

H. Glue rosebud trim along inner edge of satin ribbon on frame front.

7. **Add pastel blue satin ribbon to inside lip at picture opening.**

   Using scissors, cut a 30" length of trim. Apply dabs of white glue along inside lip of frame on one side. Position end of trim at corner so it covers inside lip and raw edges of fabric. Run glue and ribbon around remaining 3 sides. Cut ribbon at corner where ends meet and tack down with glue.

8. **Add rosebud accents at corners of picture opening on front of frame.**

   Cut off 4 roses with leaves from remaining rosebud trim. Apply dabs of white glue to 4 corners of picture opening and tack down 1 rose at each corner (illustration I).

I. Glue rosebud and leaf trim to each corner of the frame opening.

9. **Add moss green satin ribbon and roses to back of frame.**

   Place frame wrong side up on kraft paper. Using scissors, make a clean cut at end of ribbon. Position ribbon ⅜" beyond corner at upper right-hand edge of frame opening; secure to long, right-hand edge of frame opening with glue, covering raw edges of fabric, trimming ⅜" beyond corner at lower edge of frame opening. Repeat on opposite side. Using scissors, make a diagonal cut at end of remaining ribbon. Secure ribbon to the remaining sides of frame opening in the same manner, making diagonal cuts at ends of ribbon for mitered corners. Cut off 4 roses with leaves from remaining rosebud trim. Apply dabs of white glue to 4 corners of picture opening and tack down 1 rose at each corner.

Before you start, add a little sand to the rust-colored paint to exaggerate the aged effect. The finish will resemble corrosion found on metal.

WHITEWASHED IRONWORK FRAME

By Dawn Anderson

Use a paper wallpaper border and paint to simulate rusted ironwork.

The delicate tracery on this frame is not cast iron but an embossed wallpaper border. I discovered that these raised patterns lend themselves handsomely to layered painting techniques.

To turn an embossed border into rusted ironwork, you will need to paint two coats, a reddish-brown "rust" coat topped by a white coat. The whitewash effect is achieved by rubbing the white coat with neutral glaze. This step helps soften and remove some of the white paint, particularly in the raised areas, leaving behind a diffuse, hazy film that looks years instead of minutes old. Timing is important, so be sure to observe the recommended drying times before proceeding with each step.

DESIGNER'S TIP

To create the look of aged tinwork rather than rusted ironwork, substitute dark gray paint for the Burnt Sienna and Nutmeg.

MATERIALS

Makes one 18" x 18" frame

18" x 18" flat wood frame with 8" x 8" opening

4½"-wide embossed wallpaper border

1 quart clay-based vinyl wall-covering paste

FolkArt 2-oz. paints: #649 Warm White (2 bottles), #943 Burnt Sienna, #944 Nutmeg

Folk Art 8-oz. neutral glaze

Matte sealer

Beveled mirror to fit frame opening

Spring clips and screws for mounting mirror

YOU'LL ALSO NEED:

Screwdriver, clear acrylic ruler, pencil, wood block, double-sided tape, craft knife, steel ruler, three 2" foam applicators, paper towels

INSTRUCTIONS

1. Square off 4 inside corners.

   Pry hangers off frame with screwdriver or hammer and set aside. On right side, draft lines to extend each straight edge of frame opening slightly beyond corners. Tape sandpaper to wood block. Using sanding block, sand wood even with marked lines, so inside corners are square instead of curved (illustration A).

2. Paste wallpaper border to frame.

   Mark midpoint of each edge of picture opening. Rough-cut 4 lengths of wallpaper border to fit around opening, using midpoints to center design. Brush wall-covering paste on wrong side and paste borders to frame, overlapping cut ends. To miter-cut corners, align steel ruler diagonally and draw craft knife through both layers (illustration B). Remove waste, and butt together cut edges. Let dry 1 hour.

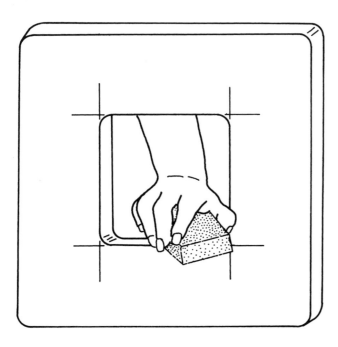

A. Use sanding block to sand wood even with marked lines, creating square inside corners.

B. Miter wallpaper at corners of frame.

3. **Paint undercoats.**

   Using foam applicator, prime entire frame with 2 coats of Warm White paint. Let dry overnight. Mix equal parts Burnt Sienna and Nutmeg. Using second foam applicator, apply 1 coat to frame. Let dry 1 hour.

4. **Create rusted appearance.**

   Apply Warm White paint to front and sides of frame. Let dry 20 minutes. Sand lightly. Working 1 embossed panel at a time, apply neutral glaze with paper towel and begin rubbing gently. Your objective is to work off some Warm White paint and expose rusty tones below. Continue just until the raised pattern becomes visible; do not "scrub" or redo areas you have rubbed previously. Paint back of frame Warm White, let dry 20 minutes, and sand lightly.

5. **Seal and finish frame.**

   Add 1 or 2 drops Nutmeg paint to a small amount of neutral glaze. Using paper towel, rub tinted glaze over back, sides, and inner edges of frame; remove excess. Let dry overnight. Using third foam applicator, apply 2 coats matte sealer, following manufacturer's instructions. Reattach frame hangers with hammer and nails. Using screwdriver and screws, attach spring clips around frame opening. Insert mirror into opening, securing in place with spring clips.

Transfer a patterned design to a wood frame using a wood-burning tool and a photocopy of your chosen image.

IMAGE-TRANSFER FRAME

By Tami D. Peterson

This frame burnished with pink dogwood blooms is surprisingly simple to make.

The elaborate dogwood floral design on this frame is actually heat-transferred directly to the frame surface with a wood-burning tool and a color photocopy of the design. I refer to this technique as color burnishing. The transferred design is made even richer with a coat of wood stain and then finished with several light coats of spray varnish.

I used a 10" x 12" unfinished hardwood frame with a 1¼" flat surface all around. You can also use a wood frame with slightly molded edges or one with a small amount of carved embellishment, depending on the motif you choose for burnishing, but a flat frame works best for all designs.

A computer and image-editing or page-layout software can be used to manipulate and size your design to your frame. Look for designs in clipart files, or use original computer-created artwork or scanned copyright-free artwork. If you don't have access to a computer with a graphics software package, you can simply use color photocopies of artwork taken from copyright-free artwork books.

There are two ways to go about this decorating technique. If you are using a computer and have an inkjet printer equipped with sublimated-dye color cartridges (see Sources on page 93), you can use designs printed directly from your inkjet printer. Otherwise you can make color photocopies of artwork, taken from a computer-generated design or from a book of copyright-free images. The actual process of burnishing is the same for both.

To burnish your design, or transfer it with heat, use a wood-burning tool with a flat tip or a very hot, vintage iron with no steam (most modern irons will not get hot enough for this purpose). If using color photocopies, be sure to experiment with the output of various color copiers available in your area. The type of toner and paper used (be sure it's regular copier paper, not iron-on or heat-transfer sheets) will affect the density of burnishing.

MATERIALS
Makes one 10" x 12" frame

10" x 12" unfinished wood frame with an 8" x 10" picture opening

Copyright-free artwork, such as clip-art files or books, original computer-created artwork, or scanned copyright-free artwork

Computer (optional)

Scanner (optional)

Inkjet printer equipped with sublimated-dye cartridges, or other printer for use with color photocopy machine (optional)

Image-editing or page-layout software (optional)

Wood-burning tool with a flat tip (or a vintage iron that heats up to 400 degrees)

Wood stain

Spray varnish

YOU'LL ALSO NEED:
Ruler, paper, scissors, painter's tape, newspaper, soft lint-free cloth, access to a color photocopy machine if using color photocopies for the transfer

INSTRUCTIONS

1. **Prepare images for transfer.**

   Measure the frame you plan to decorate. Remove glass and backing from frame; set aside. If using a computer, scan copyright-free artwork into your computer, access clip-art files or books, or create original design images as desired. Using computer graphics software package, size desired images to fit frame surfaces you plan to decorate, and then print them onto paper using an inkjet printer. You can use 1 or more images and repeat them several times around frame. Reproduce your printed images using a color photocopier, unless you have an inkjet printer equipped with sublimated dyes. If you don't have access to a computer and are using an image from a copyright-free art book, make multiple color photocopies of image as necessary to cover frame surface.

2. **Transfer designs to frame surface.**

   Preheat wood-burning tool or vintage iron for 15 minutes. Cut out your designs, leaving at least 1 edge with a ½" margin for taping. Position cutouts in pleasing pattern face down on frame. Tape each image to frame as you transfer. If using a wood-burning tool, press it firmly but briskly and evenly in small vertical movements (illustration A). If using a vintage iron, press it quickly, lifting up and down, on design (do not iron in conventional sense across design, as it may blur). Carefully peel back paper to check your work. Reposition and reheat any areas too light in color as necessary. Only remove tape once you're sure design has transferred. Transfer designs to all sides of frame in the same manner.

A. Transfer images to frame
with wood-burning tool.

3. Stain and seal frame.

Cover work surface with newspaper. Apply wood stain to the entire frame, using soft cloth and following manufacturer's instructions. This will let wood absorb moisture lost during burnishing process and give richer color to transferred images. Let dry about 30 minutes or following manufacturer's recommendations. Spray frame with several light coats of varnish (illustration B), allowing to dry between coats and following manufacturer's instructions.

B. Finish frame with several light coats of sealer.

Decorator trims give a whimsical look to this frame, and at the same time conceal fabric folds and raw edges for a neat finish.

LEOPARD-PRINT FRAME

By Genevieve A. Sterbenz

Laminate a plain wooden frame with animal-print fabric and add pompon fringe for an unexpected look.

Luxurious leopard-print fabric and coordinating trims can easily transform a plain frame into an eye-catching accessory piece. It is a perfect accent for any room, whether you make just one frame or several of different sizes. If making a collection of frames, make each of them up in different animal prints for a more interesting grouping.

I chose a velveteen leopard print because of its rich, deep color and because it has its own whimsical charm. I used a fun matching pompon trim to go around the outside of the frame and a stylish braid trim to accent both the front and back opening of the frame. Not only do the trims enhance the look of the frame but they serve a practical purpose as well. Creating clean, perfect edges with a bulky fabric like velveteen can be difficult, so I used trims to hide any raw edges that otherwise might have been visible.

When picking a frame to cover, choose one with a wide, flat surface. I found wooden frames to be readily available in stores. A wide frame will allow more of the pattern on the fabric to show, and a flat frame is always easier to work with than one with beveled edges. I have provided directions that will allow you to cover a frame of any size. To determine the amount of fabric you need, add twice the measurement of the frame width and frame depth at the outer edge to the total length of the frame to find the length of the fabric needed. Then add twice the measurement of the frame width and frame depth at the outer edge to the total width of the frame to find the width of the fabric needed. For example, start with a frame that is 8" x 10" and has a picture opening that is 5" x 7". If the width of the wooden frame from the outside edge to the inside edge is 1½" and the depth of the frame is ¼", add 1¾" to the total length and width, resulting in a 9¾" x 11¾" rectangle of fabric.

Laminating is a simple technique that will allow you to adhere the velveteen to the frame. Spray adhesive creates a smooth and lasting bond, and also allows you to reposition the fabric once or twice if needed. Velveteen tends to get bulky at the corners of the frame. An easy solution is to cut away the excess fabric in the corners before wrapping the fabric around the frame.

MATERIALS

Makes one 8" x 10" frame

⅜ yard of leopard-print velveteen

8" x 10" wooden frame with a 5" x 7" picture opening

Spray adhesive

1 yard ½"-wide black pompon fringe

1½ yards ½"-wide black braid trim

High-tack white glue

YOU'LL ALSO NEED:

Iron and ironing board, ruler, pencil, sharp scissors, kraft paper, newspaper, rotary cutter, self-healing cutting mat

INSTRUCTIONS

1. **Cut velveteen rectangle.**

   Lay velveteen wrong side up on ironing board and press with iron to remove wrinkles. Remove glass and backing from frame; set aside. Measure the depth (A) and width (B) of frame border. Add A and B together. Add twice this measurement to total length (C) and to total width (D) of the frame. This is the amount of fabric you will need (illustration A). Measure, mark, and cut a rectangle of fabric using a ruler, pencil, and scissors.

   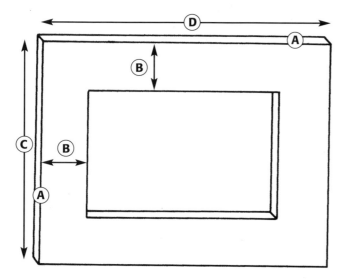

   A. 2 (A + B) + C = total length of fabric needed
   2 (A + B) + D = total width of fabric needed

2. **Laminate fabric to frame.**

   Cover work surface with kraft paper. Cover a second work surface with newspaper. Place velveteen fabric wrong side up on kraft paper. Center frame over fabric; trace around the outside and inside edges of frame with a pencil. Lift off the frame and set aside. Place velveteen wrong side up on newspaper. Apply light coat of spray adhesive to fabric. Carefully move fabric to kraft paper keeping adhe-

   sive side up. Position frame wrong side up on velvet, using penciled lines as guide. Bring 1 side of velvet up and onto back side of frame. Smooth flat. Repeat with opposite side. Using scissors, trim out excess fabric at corners and discard (illustration B). Fold down back flap and then side flap. Smooth fabric against frame to adhere (illustration C). Fold in corner fabric on remaining edge, and cut away designated area (illustration D). Repeat at remaining 3 corners of the frame. Apply scant dabs of white glue on inside flaps that were folded over. Fold up and smooth fabric flat against frame on remaining 2 sides to adhere (illustration E).

   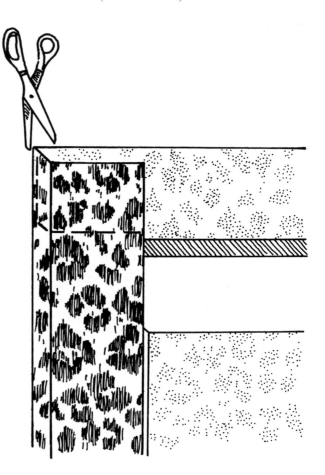

   B. Fold two opposite edges onto frame back and trim away excess at corners.

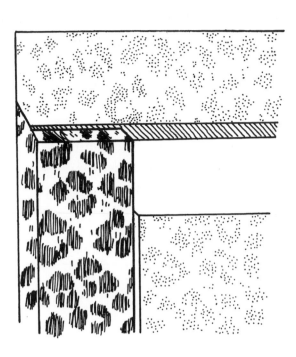

C. Fold down back and side flaps at corners.

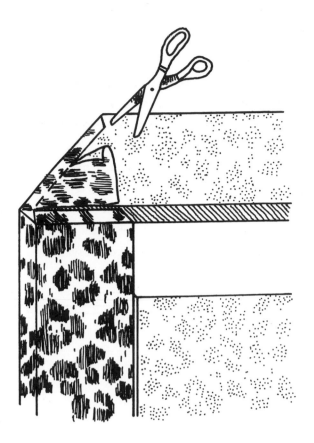

D. Trim away triangle of excess fabric at corner.

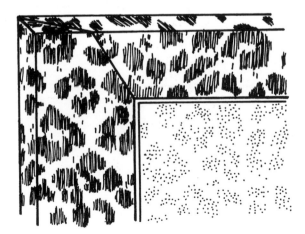

E. Fold up fabric on remaining two sides
of frame, securing to frame back.

3. Make picture opening.

Place laminated frame face down on self-healing mat. Using rotary cutter, cut fabric in frame opening diagonally from corner to corner. Repeat from opposite corners to make X-shaped cut (illustration F). Use scissors to complete cuts into corners. Bring up 1 triangular flap of fabric onto inside lip of frame. Press to adhere and smooth flat using hands. Repeat for remaining 3 sides. Use rotary cutter to trim away excess fabric from inside edge on all 4 sides (illustration G).

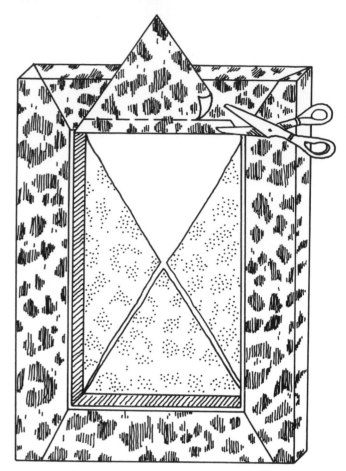

G. Fold triangular flaps to back of frame; trim excess fabric.

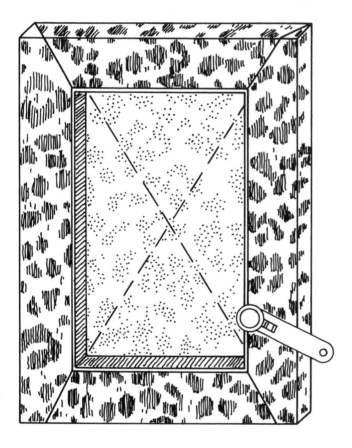

F. Cut an X through the center of the fabric on the back side.

4. Add pompon trim.

Using scissors, make clean cut at one end of trim. Turn frame so bottom end is up. Apply dabs of white glue at corner of top outside edge. Position end of trim at corner over glued area so pompons hang toward front side of frame. Run glue and trim along top outside edge (illustration H). Keep turning frame to glue trim around remaining 3 sides. Cut trim at corner where ends meet and glue down.

5. Add braid trim.

Using scissors, cut a 26" length of trim. Place frame face up on work surface. Apply dabs of white glue along one side of inner lip of frame. Starting at corner, position trim over lip of frame with remaining width of trim overlapping onto front of frame (illustration I). Run glue and trim around remaining 3 sides. Cut trim at corner where ends meet and tack down with glue.

6. **Add braid trim to back of frame.**

Using scissors, cut a 26" length of trim. Place frame wrong side up on work surface. Apply dabs of white glue along one inner edge of frame over raw edges. Position end of trim at corner and press trim to glued area to adhere. Edge of trim should be flush with edge of frame opening. Continue adding glue and trim around remaining 3 sides, turning trim at corners. Cut trim at corner where ends meet and tack down with glue.

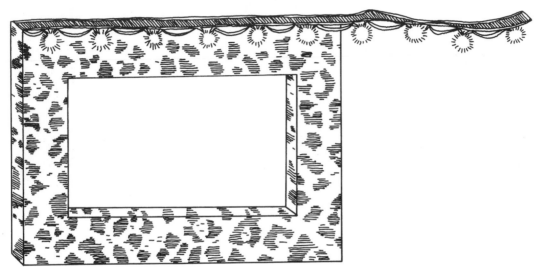

H. Add pompon fringe to outer edge of frame, securing with glue.

I. Glue braid trim over inner edge of frame.

This finish is created by layering pearlized foil
over an ivory base coat.

MOTHER-OF-PEARL WEDDING FRAME

By Sandra Salamony

Coat an oval frame with a shimmering iridescent finish.

Create a delicate, translucent mother-of-pearl finish on an oval frame that is perfect for wedding invitations or pictures. The sheer, lustrous ribbons complement the iridescent finish and add colors reminiscent of bridesmaids in June.

The oval frame I used was made by the Old Schwamb Mill, a nonprofit, charitable educational organization in Arlington, Massachusetts. First built in 1650, the mill was converted in 1864 to a manufactory dedicated to producing the highest quality hand-turned oval and circular picture frames and picture frame molding. The mill is still producing frames today, using the original machinery, tools, and techniques favored by five generations of Schwambs and their employees. It is listed in the National Register of Historic Places and is supported by gifts, grants, contributions, and earned income. Frames made at Old Schwamb Mill can be found in museums, galleries, and private homes throughout the country, including the White House.

This oval frame can be ordered from the mill for $50. For a less expensive alternative, substitute a similarly sized unfinished oval frame.

MATERIALS

Makes one 6½" x 8½" oval frame
6½" x 8½" oval frame with
    5" x 7" oval picture opening
Delta Renaissance Foil Mother-of-
    Pearls kit: sealer, light ivory
    paint, adhesive, pearlized foil
Four ¾" brass turn buttons
5" x 7" celadon mat with 3" x 5"
    oval opening
⅛"-thick foamcore board
1"-wide sheer ribbon:
    2½ yards pink
    2½ yards light olive
Small brass brads
Thin gold wires

YOU'LL ALSO NEED:
Foam brushes, hammer, pencil, craft knife, cutting mat, scissors, ruler

INSTRUCTIONS

1. **Prepare frame and inserts.**

   Remove glass and backing from frame; set aside. Using foam brush, apply sealer to all frame surfaces. Dry 30 minutes. Nail 4 turn buttons to back of frame, spacing them evenly around edge of opening. Using glass oval as a see-through template, mark and cut wedding invitation or photograph to match. Also mark 1 oval on mat and 3 ovals on foamcore; cut out with craft knife. Draft smaller oval on 1 foamcore oval ¾" in from edge all around. Cut out and discard interior, leaving an oval ring.

2. **Apply pearlized finish.**

   Read kit manufacturer's instructions. Using foam brush, apply 2 coats ivory paint to front and sides of frame, letting dry 30 minutes after each coat. Next, apply thin coat of adhesive to same areas. Let dry 15 minutes, or until adhesive turns clear. Apply second coat. Let dry 1 hour, or until tacky. Cut pearlized foil into small rectangles, slightly wider than width of frame. Press pearlized foil, shiny side up, against frame, covering as large a section as is manageable. Rub with your fingers and then peel off the foil to reveal the pearl finish left behind (illustration A). Repeat process until frame is completely pearlized. Let dry overnight. Apply 1 sealer coat and let dry.

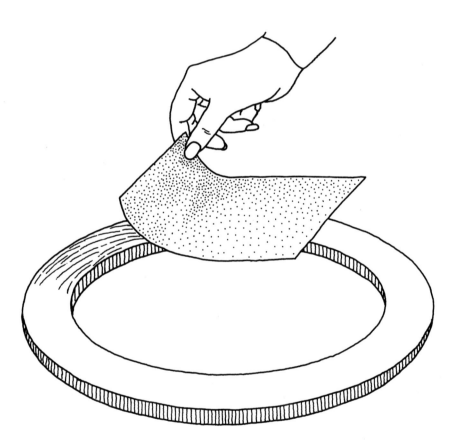

A. Press pearlized foil against adhesive-covered frame; then remove foil to reveal finish.

3. Add ribbons.

Hold both ribbons together and cut 18" length. Using brads, tack ends to back of frame at each side to make ribbon hanger. Fold each remaining length into a 6-loop bow (illustration B). Wire both bows together. Nail to top of frame with brad.

4. Assemble frame.

Insert pieces into frame from back in this order: glass, matt, foamcore ring, oval invitation or photo, 2 foamcore ovals. Check placement from right side; close turn buttons.

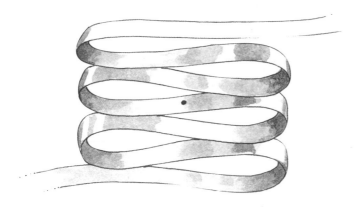

DESIGNER'S TIP

For a deeper abalone finish, use the black basecoat paint that comes in the Mother-of-Pearl kit. Try the foil over your own dark blue paint to create the effect of paua shell.

B. Fold ribbon in half to locate middle. Observing midpoint, fold.

Silver-lined seed beads give this frame extra sparkle. Seed beads with silver linings are available in a wide variety of colors.

BEADED FRAME

By Patty Cox

Create an elegant beaded frame with some seed beads, spool wire, and perforated paper.

This elegant-looking frame is quite easy to make with seed beads and a perforated paper base. You can alter the directions to make the sides longer if you like.

The perforated paper guide is the secret to achieving an accurate frame width on all sides of the frame. Maintain frame width by making stitches eighteen holes apart in the paper. For each stitch, come up on one side of the frame width, string enough beads onto the wire to cover eighteen holes across the paper, and then insert the wire into a hole to the back side. Carry the wire across the back and repeat in the next set of holes. Gradually increase or decrease beads to make mitered corners. It is not necessary to count the number of beads on each stitch. Since the sizes of the beads vary, you may use a different number of beads in each row. You will need to count beads only for the mitered corners.

Once you string the beads onto the paper, fold the excess paper to the back of the beadwork and add a ribbon-covered cardboard backing. Create a recessed place for a photo with craft sticks glued along three sides of the center opening on the back side. If desired, cut a piece of clear acetate to fit the frame opening to protect your photo.

MATERIALS
Makes one 4½" x 4½" frame
14-count perforated paper
34-gauge silver spool wire
Blue seed beads (2 hanks)
4⅜" x 4⅜" square cardboard
¾ yd. 1½"-wide ribbon
6 mini craft sticks, ¼" wide x
    3" long

YOU'LL ALSO NEED:
Pencil, craft knife, tacky glue, glue stick, large books, embroidery floss

INSTRUCTIONS

1. **Draft pattern on perforated paper.**

   Draft frame base pattern on perforated paper. Count 5 holes from edge of paper to use as outer margin. Draft inner and outer dimensions of frame base on perforated paper, allowing 18 holes for each frame side and 31 holes for frame center. Mark diagonal lines through opposite corners of the frame pattern (illustration A).

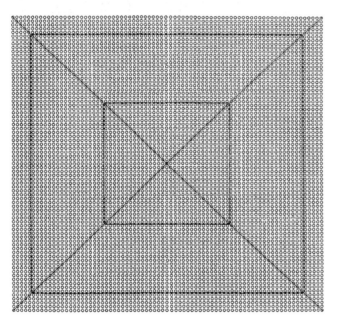

   A. Draw frame dimensions and then draw diagonal lines through opposite corners.

2. **Bead frame.**

   Cut a 30" length 34-gauge wire. Insert one end through top left corner hole (1) of pattern drawn on perforated paper. Bend a 2" tail to the back side. String 1 bead onto wire. Insert wire end through hole 2. Bring wire end up through next hole (3) along upper edge of frame base pattern. Add a bead. Return wire through hole below (4). Then bring wire up at 5, add 2 beads and insert wire through hole at 6 (illustration B, top). Continue

stitching wire vertically, adding a bead with each stitch (illustration B, bottom) until you reach the inner marked frame line. The vertical wire stitches should cover and secure the 2" wire tail on the frame back. Continue beading across the top of the frame, stitching from the outer marked line to the inner marked line. Repeat beading at corner as for first corner. To end wire, insert a 2" tail under previous stitches on back.

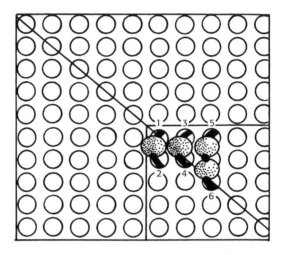

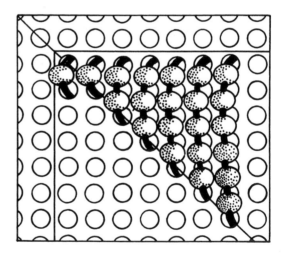

   B. Use wire to stitch beads between inner and outer frame lines.

Bead the bottom of the frame as for the top of the frame. Bead the left side of the frame, using illustration C as a guide for mitering the corner. Complete the frame sides following the penciled pattern.

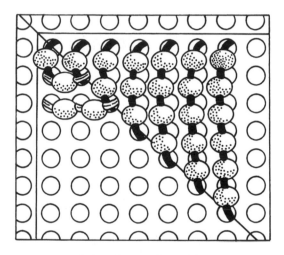

C. Stitch beads to sides of frame, mitering corners as indicated.

3. Finish frame.

Cut an X through unstitched center of perforated paper using craft knife. Fold each edge of paper to back. Fold outer edges to back, mitering corners (illustration D). Secure paper folds with glue stick. Mark an X on 4⅜" cardboard square (frame backing). Draft 2¼" square in the center; cut out square using craft knife. Glue 1½"-wide ribbon over each side of frame backing. Fold and glue edges to wrong side. Glue covered frame backing to wrong side of beaded frame. Place frame between large books until glue dries. Use tacky glue to glue 3 mini craft sticks on frame back, ⅛" from the center opening on three sides. Glue 3 mini craft sticks across opening, securing to side sticks to hold photo in place (illustration E). Allow glue to dry. Mark top center of frame back. Stitch a hanging loop using embroidery floss.

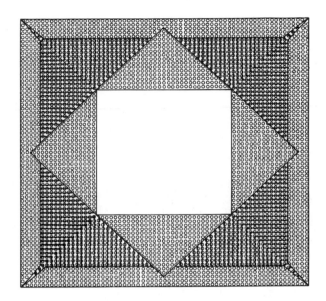

D. Fold excess paper to back side. Miter outer corners and secure with gluestick.

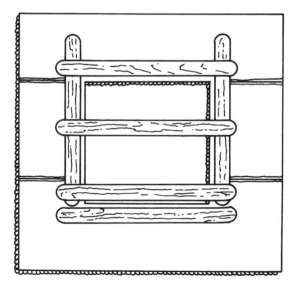

E. Glue craft sticks around inner edge of frame back and across opening.

The vintage look of this frame is achieved by
applying a dark brown glazing medium over gold
foil. Use an old piece of jewelry chain to accent
the frame and maintain the vintage appearance.

GILDED-AND-JEWELED FRAME

By Livia McRee

Make a custom-sized frame from balsa wood and dollhouse molding strips, and then embellish it with gold leaf and jewelry findings for a distinctive look.

The rich tones of this gilded frame are complemented by strands of gold-toned chains and dangling beads. A gold picture ring at the top is used for hanging the frame and adds to the charm of the piece.

The frame base is constructed from a 6" wide plank of balsa wood, making it easy to create a custom-sized frame for a special photo. The delicately detailed dollhouse moldings that accent the base are easily cut with a craft and hobby miter box.

Once you construct it, give the frame its gold finish with a layer of adhesive and gold craft foil and rub stain over the finish to give it a richer tone. Secure a few lengths of jewelry chain and some accent beads to the frame with three small screw eyes.

MATERIALS

Makes one 6" x 8" frame

³⁄₁₆" x 6" x 36" plank of balsa wood (standard size)

Tacky glue

Four ½" x 24" dollhouse molding strips

Two ¼" x 24" dollhouse molding strips

Aleene's foiling glue

Aleene's gold craft foil

Dark brown translucent glazing medium

Satin acrylic varnish

3 small gold-toned screw eyes

24" of gold-toned chain

5 gold-toned jump rings, 5mm

3 gold-toned head pins

Assorted 7mm and 9mm beads

3 gold-toned jump rings, 3mm

Gold-toned picture ring

3¾" x 5¾" piece of glass or acetate

3¾" x 5¾" piece of foamcore board or cardboard for picture backing

YOU'LL ALSO NEED:

Fine sandpaper, spray mister, paper towels, small hobby saw, miter box, soft-bristled brush, wire cutters, round-nosed pliers, linen framing tape or masking tape

INSTRUCTIONS

1. **Make frame base.**

   Cut two 6" x 8" pieces from balsa wood. Using a craft knife with a sharp blade, cut a 4" x 6" rectangle in center of one piece, leaving a 1" border on all sides. Cut a 3½" x 5½" rectangle in center of remaining piece. Secure frame pieces together with glue, aligning the outer edges. This will create a recessed area for a piece of glass or acetate, the photo, and a backing material (illustration A). When glue dries, sand any rough or uneven spots on frame. Remove sanding dust with a misted paper towel.

   A. Secure frame pieces, creating a recessed area for glass and photo.

2. **Cut molding strips and glue into position.**

   Measure exact length of side edges of frame and cut 4 strips for sides, using a hobby saw. Make sure edges will abut. Glue strips to edges of frame; sand corners. Measure length and width of frame again to get precise measurement needed for 4 outer-border strips. Cut ½" molding for outer border to determined measurements with a miter box and hobby saw; be sure the 45-degree angle of mitered

   strip is facing the right way. Sand ends of strips lightly, if necessary. Glue outer-border strips to outer edges of frame. Measure sides of picture opening for inner border. Cut ¼" molding to determined measurements as before. Glue strips around inner edge of frame around picture opening (illustration B).

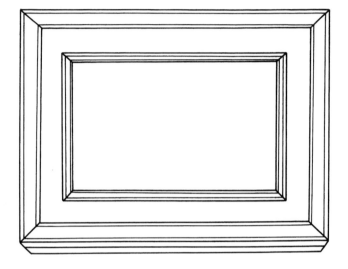

   B. Glue molding strips to the inner and outer edges of the frame.

3. **Gild, antique, and varnish frame.**

   Coat frame with an even layer of foiling glue. The glue should not be spread too thinly or thickly; allow to dry until the glue becomes transparent. Press the foil onto the frame, following the manufacturer's instructions, and burnish with your fingers. Ease the foil into crevices with your fingernail. Reapply the foil if necessary until the frame is mostly gilded, but do not add more glue. Next, use a soft-bristled brush to paint dark brown translucent glazing medium over the whole frame. This will color any areas not covered by foil. When the glaze is dry, apply 2 coats of satin varnish to the frame to seal it; allow to dry between coats.

4. Add beaded chain accent.

First, attach screw eyes to the center bottom of the frame at the far left, far right, and center of the frame. Next, cut two 3½" and two 3¾" lengths of chain. Join one end of 1 long and 1 short chain to the center screw eye with a 5mm jump ring. Join the remaining ends of the chains to the left screw eye with a 5mm jump ring (illustration C). Repeat with the remaining 2 chains on the right side (illustration D). Next, thread a couple of beads on a head pin and clip the wire, leaving ½" length of wire above the beads; bend wire over at 90-degree angle. Bend the excess wire into a small loop at the top using round-nosed pliers. Repeat to make another identical beaded drop (illustration E). Cut two ¾" lengths of chain and attach 1 to each of the beaded drops using 3mm jump rings. Attach each short chain with beaded drop to the 5mm jump ring secured to the end screw eyes. Finally, create the center beaded drop in the same manner using 3 beads and 1" of chain. Secure to the center screw eye using the last 5mm jump ring (illustration F). Center and screw the picture ring to the top of the frame.

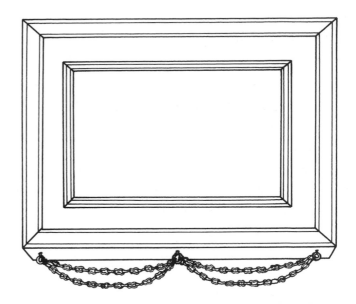

D. Secure chains to lower edge of frame

E. Create beaded drops by threading beads onto a head pin and finishing with a wire loop at the top.

C. Join the two lengths of chain to the screw eyes with a jump ring.

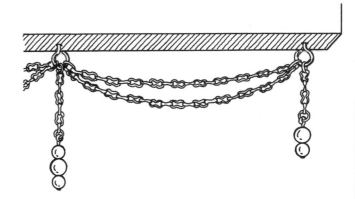

F. Attach beaded drops to chain and screw eyes with jump rings.

5. Insert glass or acetate, picture, and foamcore or cardboard into recessed opening on back of frame. Secure with linen or masking tape.

gilded-and-jeweled frame

Wallpaper borders add color and pattern to
plain wooden frames.

WALLPAPER-COVERED FRAMES

By Lily Franklin

Transform any flat frame using prepasted wallpaper borders and a special corner treatment.

Common wallpaper borders can transform a plain frame into a decorative accessory that matches or complements your home's decor. You can use one border to decorate several frames of different sizes, or you can mix and match coordinated prints, plaids, stripes, and geometrics to group several mis-matched frames. With the variety of wallpaper border designs and colors available today, the choices are almost limitless.

For this project, you'll need to make two choices: the type of frame and the design of the wallpaper border. I recommend selecting a frame with flat, broad surfaces or, at the most, smooth and gentle troughs or crests that will allow the wallpaper to lie flat. Frames with carved designs or deep contours will not work. When choosing a border pattern, look for one that can be hung easily in four different directions. A landscape pattern might look odd hanging upside down, but geometrics, dots, stripes, or florals might be more flexible.

You'll also need to consider the scale of the design. A wide frame can accommodate large-scale patterns, while a narrow frame will look more attractive with smaller prints. Patterns that include straight lines or bands of color on each side of the central design area can be used as guides for more accurate cutting and for neat placement on the frame. Some patterns have an interior design space bordered by two or more parallel stripes of color, which you can adapt to different frame widths. Stripes and straight lines can also be used to define the edges of the frame visually.

The frames shown were made with prepasted wallpaper borders. If you cannot find a prepasted border to your liking, you can use paper-backed borders, but you will need to purchase wallpaper paste. Follow the manufac-turer's recommendations for the best results. For other design variations, consider using leftover scraps of wallpaper, textured wallcoverings such as burlap or grasscloth, or cork, although the latter requires a special premixed adhesive.

MATERIALS

Makes 1 frame
Prepasted wallpaper border
Picture frame with flat, wide
    border

YOU'LL ALSO NEED:

Scissors, self-healing cutting mat, clear acrylic grid ruler, craft knife, pencil, steel straightedge, waxed paper, sponge

To apply the wallpaper, cut the border to fit the frame, and then miter and glue down the corners. The trick is in the corner treatment. I recommend that you practice cutting 45-degree beveled pieces of border and then overlay them into the desired design. Angle-cut two of the border pieces ¼" larger to allow for an overlap at the mitered corners. You may have to slide the pattern back and forth to find the right pattern fit. If you can't arrange the design so it matches perfectly, select one motif and decoupage it on top of the seam to conceal the corners. You can trim the wallpaper border even with the edge of the frame, or if you prefer, fold the extra allowance onto the side of the frame, using hospital folds to finish the corners neatly.

INSTRUCTIONS

1. **Test-fit border design.**

   Remove glass and backing from frame; set aside. Cut small piece of wallpaper border off end of roll for testing. Position test piece on flat section of frame, adjust design position, and then crease at inner and outer frame edges (illustration A).

2. **Prepare border for cutting.**

   Unroll wallpaper border on cutting mat. Position top of frame face down on border design so inner and outer frame edges correspond to creases made in test piece from step 1. If design is symmetrical, adjust so designs visible to left and right of outer frame edges match. Run craft-knife blade from inner frame corners down to lower edge of border. Mark small dots on border at outer frame corners. Cut border from roll beyond marked area (illustration B) and label back as "top." Repeat to mark, cut, and label border sections for left side, bottom, and right side of frame.

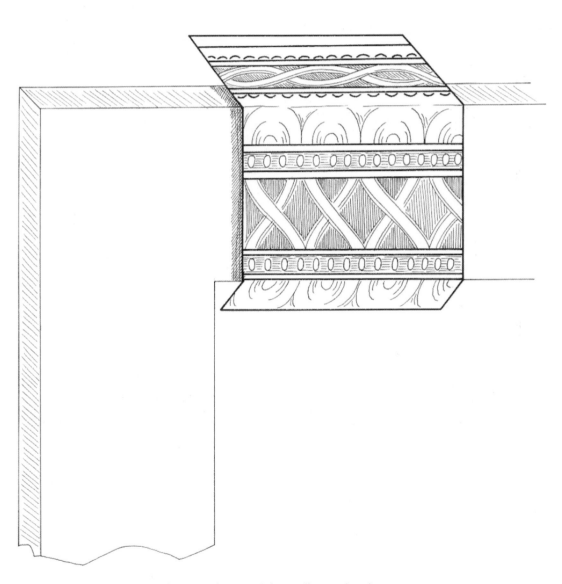

A. Fold a sample cut of the wallpaper border over the frame to decide how the design should fall.

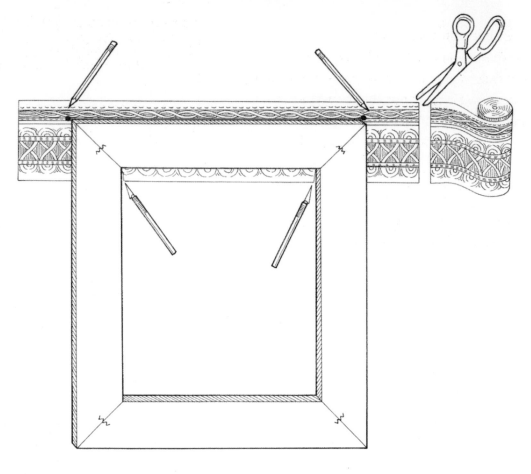

B. Turn the frame face down and use it as a template to mark and cut the border paper.

3. **Miter-cut 4 border sections.**

Lay 2 side sections of cut wallpaper border face up. At each end, draft diagonal line from end of slit through dot made in step 2 (illustration C). Lay top and bottom sections face up. At each end, lay ruler diagonally from end of slit through dot; then adjust ruler position down ¼" and draft line (illustration D). Using straightedge and craft knife, cut on marked lines of all sections and discard excess.

C. Use the markings to draft diagonal lines for cutting.

D. Provide a ¼" allowance when cutting the miters on the top and bottom sections.

4. Trim excess from outer edge.

Lay each section of wallpaper border face up. Using straightedge and pencil, mark line corresponding to outer crease made in test piece from step 1. Using straightedge and craft knife, cut on marked line of each section and discard excess (illustration E).

E. Trim off the outer edge of each section even with your folded sample.

5. Glue sections to frame.

Turn each section face down on waxed paper. Using moist sponge, wet entire back surface, going out beyond edges. Wet edges will curl; when they relax (1 to 2 minutes), position section on frame so design placement at inner and outer frame edges corresponds to creases made in test piece from step 1. Fold excess at inner edge onto frame inner lip; then turn frame over and trim off any excess with craft knife. Press firmly on right side with damp sponge to ensure adhesion and remove air bubbles. Glue bottom section in the same way (illustration F), and then glue sides (illustration G).

F. Glue the top and bottom sections to the frame first.

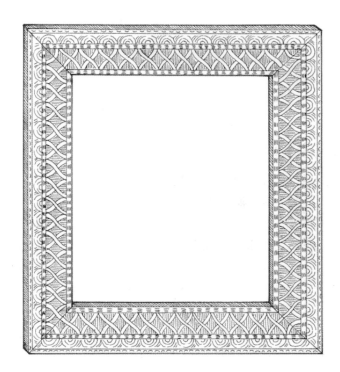

G. Glue the side sections in place. The miters will overlap at the corners for a tight join.

Black paint rubbed over the surface of the
frame helps to define the design.

EMBOSSED PEWTER FRAME

By Marisa Zvorak

Create a metal frame with a raised surface design from a sheet of pewter and a few styling tools.

This highly ornate frame was created from an unfinished wood frame, a sheet of pewter, and a few embossing tools, all available from craft stores. The blackened finish was achieved with a final wash of acrylic paint.

You will emboss the design onto the pewter sheet in stages. For best results, stretch the pewter little by little by pressing on it with a stylus; then make the impressions deeper with hardwood modeling tools. Once you emboss the design, fill the raised area with wood putty on the back side to maintain the design. Then you can glue and trim the pewter sheet to fit around the wood frame. The embossed design has a motif centered on one short side. You may use this side as either the top or bottom of the frame.

I applied a black paint wash to this frame to help bring out the design. The paint settles in the crevices giving definition to the piece. You may also leave the frame a natural pewter color if you wish.

MATERIALS

Makes one 6½" x 8" frame
9¼" x 12" sheet of pewter
6½" x 8" wood frame with
    3½" x 5" picture opening
Black acrylic paint

YOU'LL ALSO NEED:

Pattern (page 92), access to a photocopy machine, tape, 9" x 12" sheet of thick glass, double-ended ball-point stylus, 9" x 12" sheet of felt, hardwood modeling tools, wood putty, carving spatula or small knife, paper towels, contact cement, craft knife, fine steel wool, soft cloth

INSTRUCTIONS

1. Prepare pattern.

Photocopy pattern (page 92) and tape to right side of pewter sheet. Place pewter sheet on glass surface. Trace over the paper design with a ball-point stylus to transfer image to pewter sheet. Remove pattern.

2. Emboss pewter sheet.

Place pewter right side down on felt. With stylus, press down on pewter, following contour of design lines; do small sections of design at a time. Turn pewter sheet over and remove felt. Press lightly around raised contours of design on front side (illustration A). Repeat in this manner for remaining sections of design. With front of pewter sheet down on felt, press areas of design inside contour lines, using hardwood modeling tools to raise design even more (illustration B). Turn pewter sheet right side up and lightly flatten any remaining surface that has not been embossed. Press around all contour lines with stylus to create perfect outline.

A. Press lightly around raised contours on the front side with a stylus.

B. Press hardwood modeling tools on the back side to raise the design; then press around the contour lines on the front side with a stylus.

3. Fill raised area with putty.

Place pewter right side down on felt. On back side of pewter sheet, fill in raised areas with wood putty, using a carving spatula or small knife; be careful to keep the filler in the raised areas only. Use a wet paper towel to clean all the flat areas and wipe away any filler. Allow to dry.

4. Secure pewter sheet to frame.

Turn design right side up and flatten non-embossed areas using hardwood modeling tool. Remove glass and backing from frame; set aside. Center design over frame front and secure in place with contact cement. Push on center of pewter to stretch pewter and to cover inside edge of frame. Cut off excess pewter with a craft knife. Fold pewter over outside edges of frame, pressing the pewter sheet against the edge of the frame with the hardwood modeling tool for a smooth fit. Glue pewter to inside and outside edges of frame, trimming off any excess pewter with craft knife.

5. Finishing.

With stylus, go over all non-embossed areas on front of frame, using a small circular motion to engrave them. Using stylus, score vertical lines along outside edges of frame and around frame opening (illustration C). Use a piece of fine steel wool to rub entire design very lightly. Apply black acrylic paint to surface of frame with soft cloth and wipe away excess, leaving paint in cracks and recessed areas only for an antiqued effect.

C. Using a stylus, engrave front of frame using a circular motion. Score vertical lines along the inner and outer edges.

SOURCES

Conde Systems
800-826-6332
www.conde.com
*sublimated-dye color printer
    cartridges and inkjet printers*

Epson
800-873-7766
www.epson.com
*inkjet printers, scanners, and
    specialty inkjet papers*

Mosaic Mercantile
877-9-MOSAIC
www.mosaicmercantile.com
tile and tools

Old Schwamb Mill
781-643-0554
www.oldschwambmill.org
frames

Pearl Paint
800-221-6845 x2297
www.pearlpaint.com
dollhouse moldings

Rockler Woodworking and Hardware
800-279-4441
www.rockler.com
darkening solution

Sechtem's Wood Products Inc.
800-255-4285
www.tolemine.com
*unfinished wood frames, including
    square mirror frame, 18" x 18"*

CONTRIBUTORS

Floral-Beaded Tulle Frame
Designer: Genevieve A. Sterbenz
Illustrator: Jil Johänson
Photographer: Bill Lindner

Studded Velvet Frames
Designer: Mary Ann Hall
Illustrator: Mary Newell DePalma
Photographer: Carl Tremblay

Marquetry Frame
Designer: Livia McRee
Illustrator: Jil Johänson
Photographer: Bill Lindner

Faux Ebony and Ivory Marquetry Frame
Designer: Lily Franklin
Illustrator: Judy Love
Photographer: Carl Tremblay

Mosaic Mirror Frame
Designer: Jill MacKay
Illustrator: Jil Johänson
Photographer: Bill Lindner

Mosaic Picture Frame
Designer: Jill MacKay
Illustrator: Jil Johänson
Photographer: Bill Lindner

Cherry Triptych Frame

Designer: Sandra Salamony

Illustrator: Jil Johänson

Photographer: Carl Tremblay

Weathered Wood Frame

Designer: Patty Cox

Illustrator: Jil Johänson

Photographer: Bill Lindner

Checked-Silk Frame

Designer: Genevieve A. Sterbenz

Illustrator: Jil Johänson

Photographer: Bill Lindner

Whitewashed Ironwork Frame

Designer: Dawn Anderson

Illustrator: Jil Johänson

Photographer: Carl Tremblay

Image-Transfer Frame

Designer: Tami D. Peterson

Illustrator: Jil Johänson

Photographer: Bill Lindner

Leopard-Print Frame

Designer: Genevieve A. Sterbenz

Illustrator: Jil Johänson

Photographer: Bill Lindner

Mother-of-Pearl Wedding Frame

Designer: Sandra Salamony

Illustrators: Jil Johänson and Judy Love

Photographer: Carl Tremblay

Beaded Frame

Designer: Patty Cox

Illustrator: Jil Johänson

Photographer: Bill Lindner

Gilded-and-Jeweled Frame

Designer: Livia McRee

Illustrator: Jil Johänson

Photographer: Bill Lindner

Wallpaper-Covered Frames

Designer: Lily Franklin

Illustrator: Mary Newell DePalma

Photographer: Carl Tremblay

Embossed Pewter Frame

Designer: Marisa Zvorak

Illustrator: Jil Johänson

Photographer: Bill Lindner

new and bestselling titles from

America's Best-Loved Craft & Hobby Books™

America's Best-Loved Quilt Books®

NEW RELEASES
Bear's Paw Plus
All Through the Woods
American Quilt Classics
Amish Wall Quilts
Animal Kingdom CD-ROM
Batik Beauties
The Casual Quilter
Fantasy Floral Quilts
Fast Fusible Quilts
Friendship Blocks
From the Heart
Log Cabin Fever
Machine-Stitched Cathedral Stars
Magical Hexagons
Quilts From Larkspur Farm
Potting Shed Patchwork
Repliqué Quilts
Successful Scrap Quilts
  From Simple Rectangles

CRAFTS
The Art of Stenciling
Baby Dolls and Their Clothes
Creating with Paint
The Decorated Kitchen
The Decorated Porch
A Handcrafted Christmas
Painted Chairs
Sassy Cats

APPLIQUÉ
Artful Album Quilts
Artful Appliqué
Colonial Appliqué
Red and Green: An Appliqué Tradition
Rose Sampler Supreme

BABY QUILTS
Easy Paper-Pieced Baby Quilts
Even More Quilts for Baby: Easy as ABC
More Quilts for Baby: Easy as ABC
Play Quilts
The Quilted Nursery
Quilts for Baby: Easy as ABC

HOLIDAY QUILTS
Christmas at That Patchwork Place
Holiday Collage Quilts
Paper Piece a Merry Christmas
A Snowman's Family Album Quilt
Welcome to the North Pole

LEARNING TO QUILT
Basic Quiltmaking Techniques for:
  Borders and Bindings
  Divided Circles
  Hand Appliqué
  Machine Appliqué
  Strip Piecing
The Joy of Quilting
The Simple Joys of Quilting
Your First Quilt Book (or it should be!)

ROTARY CUTTING
101 Fabulous Rotary-Cut Quilts
365 Quilt Blocks a Year Perpetual Calendar
Around the Block Again
Biblical Blocks
Creating Quilts with Simple Shapes
Flannel Quilts
More Fat Quarter Quilts
More Quick Watercolor Quilts
Razzle Dazzle Quilts

SCRAP QUILTS
Nickel Quilts
Scrap Frenzy
Scrappy Duos
Spectacular Scraps

PAPER PIECING
50 Fabulous Paper-Pieced Stars
For the Birds
Paper Piece a Flower Garden
Paper-Pieced Bed Quilts
Paper-Pieced Curves
A Quilter's Ark
Show Me How to Paper Piece

KNITTING & CROCHET
Too Cute!
Clever Knits
Crochet for Babies and Toddlers
Crocheted Sweaters
Fair Isle Sweaters Simplified
Irresistible Knits
Knit It Your Way
Knitted Shawls, Stoles, and Scarves
Knitted Sweaters for Every Season
Knitting with Novelty Yarns
Paintbox Knits
Simply Beautiful Sweaters
Simply Beautiful Sweaters for Men
The Ultimate Knitter's Guide

Our books are available at bookstores and your favorite craft, fabric and yarn retailers. If you don't see the title you're looking for, visit us at www.martingale-pub.com or contact us at:

1-800-426-3126

International: 1-425-483-3313

Fax: 1-425-486-7596

E-mail: info@martingale-pub.com

For more information and a full list of our titles, visit our Web site or call for a free catalog.